Food Fun Love

Pauline Parry

Food
Fun
Love

Party Styles

PHOTOGRAPHY BY WILL HENSHALL

I want to dedicate this book to my mum and dad
who gave me many guiding words but these in particular:

In life you have to work hard and play hard – otherwise it is no life at all.

First published in 2009 by Catersource, Minneapolis, Minnesota
Published in 2022 by Pauline Parry, in partnership with whitefox publishing

www.wearewhitefox.com

ISBN 978-1-915036-30-8
Also available as an ebook
ISBN 978-1-915036-29-2

Design and Art Direction by Nan Hildebrandt
Editorial Assistance by Pauline Hoogmoed
Production Assistance by Andrea Klaassen
Photographs by Will Henshall, Henshall Photography
Cover design by Siulen Design
Project management by whitefox
Printed and bound by CPI Group (UK) Ltd, Croydon CR0 4YY

CONTENTS

INTRODUCTION

This book is called Food, Fun, Love and that title absolutely reflects my lifestyle and my work. Food is where it all begins and that's where my passion lies. The fun is how I create an environment and an ambience for guests, whether I am entertaining at my home or doing an event or party for a client. The love is quite simply the love of doing what I do and sharing this love with friends, family and ultimately, my clients.

As I began working on this book, it was quite clear I wanted to show different environments, I wanted energy, I wanted to prepare food that was right for the occasion and I wanted to have each chapter include the people that have come into my life in one way or another and share this experience with me. After all, this was nearly a year of my life and I wanted it to be an outstanding memory for always. What I did not want was to have a book with staged table environments, in pretty settings, with over-the-top food (that might be unrealistic for most to cook), and that had no real action taking place. Parties are all about people sharing life, enjoying conversation, company, food and beverage, and giving the time together a sense of occasion.

In each chapter, I've detailed how the party came about and introduce you to the main characters in each event, their friends and other important people in their lives. It truly was an amazing journey – the pleasure I receive from touching other people's lives gives me so much joy. I cannot help but reflect on how fortunate I am to be able to bring wonderful celebrations to people in the work that I do. So once again it is the Food, Fun, Love that constantly appears to be what my life is all about!

While this book is all about me, I could not possibly have taken on this project without the support of my staff at Good Gracious! Events. We are truly a team of people who inspire each other. We all have different layers of creativity and talent. When planning, we usually take time to brainstorm over an hour or two until all the elements and pieces come together. Then we all scatter in our different directions to plan the various details assigned to each one of us, and then we harmonize the details for the party. I might add, I have found that creativity doesn't always happen when it should. While these brainstorming gatherings are good and give us direction, more often than not it continues to develop right up to the time of the party. There are many times when I wake up in the middle of the night and have a vision that changes the course of

continued >

of action and this change continues right up to when the party begins! I wish it was as simple as black and white but it isn't. I want to take a moment to tell you about the Good Gracious! team that is very important to me.

Margarita has been with me since day one when she washed dishes and spoke no English. She is now my Executive Chef – that says it all.

Martha was a single parent who joined us right at the very beginning doing prep work. She is now Vice President.

Joanne, our Chef de Cuisine, is my daughter. We have worked together for 12 years, day in and day out. Although not perfect every day, we certainly have found pleasure in working together and I personally have enjoyed watching her grow into the chef she is today – magic!

Ernesto, Ben, Rosie, Irma and Gabina are the strength that keeps our product the best it can possibly be.

Mary, our bookkeeper has been with GG! from the start. Not an easy job, and no doubt she can tell you some business stories!

And Dan, a fairly new addition to the fold, slipped right in with his talent, loyalty and creativity. There are many more who know who they are, that are filtering right in with the Good Gracious! spirit.

This team did not happen overnight but because of their creativity, work ethic and loyalty each will always be cherished in my heart and at Good Gracious! and this book is as much about them as it is about me.

Last but not least, my husband Dennis, plays an extremely important role in my life even though we do not work together. He lends his ear to all of my ups and downs, listens to my ideas about putting a party together, tastes the food at all hours of the day (which is not such a bad thing usually, but lamb chop with a demi glaze rosemary sauce first thing in the morning is not his idea of breakfast). He might not agree when I take crazy risks but he is always there regardless if the results are good or bad. He builds me tables, risers and any other item I might need for an event without question, even on an hour's notice. He allows me the freedom to grow and to be who I am. Without his support I would not be who I am today and this book would not have happened. Oh, I nearly forgot, we also share a lot of laughter and wine together!

Wishing you a life filled with Food, Fun and LOVE!

THE

GOOD SPELL
BOOK

LOVE CHARMS
MAGICAL CURES
AND
OTHER PRACTICAL
SORCERY

PAULINE

GOOD SPELL NIGHT
At home with friends

I have always been interested in the idea that the power of ancient spirits exists and that it can give us the energy and ability to create positive change in our lives and the lives of those around us.

One day when wandering into a book store, a book of good spells caught my eye. I immediately thought it would be perfect to have a party based on this book and on the notion of good spells. After all, I believe that casting good spells is what we do over people when we bring them together for a meal.

The look of the book, with its deep red fabric cover, was my inspiration for the color scheme of the table. And because my home is Spanish in style, I chose a menu influenced by the cuisine of Spain.

A book was placed at each setting. I added my guests' names to each book very easily, with a label maker and a gold label. That little detail was so effective in creating the first good spell – breaking the ice!

Before the party, I had chosen three spells from the book – one for love, one for health and one for wealth – and provided all the elements those spells took to perform (according to the book, a candle, a penny and a key) and placed them in a decorative bag for each guest. During the evening, we performed each spell as directed by the book. I'm sure you can see where this is going – dinner was a riot, with interesting conversation brought on by the spells...and the Rioja wine helped too!

It made me think about the nature of dinner parties. Really, we – the host and the guests – are the entertainment for the evening. But, because people have somewhat forgotten the fine art of conversation, *The Good Spell Book* gave this group a structure for their conversation, for the entertainment really. It enabled us to share time with one another in a completely different way. Now that is what I call a powerful energy!

To me, this is the essence of great entertaining – bringing out the best in people with food, fun and love to create a moment in time that is remembered forever. In the "spirit" of this evening of giving, each guest was given a copy of the book and their bag of goodies so they could continue to practice some good spells on their own.

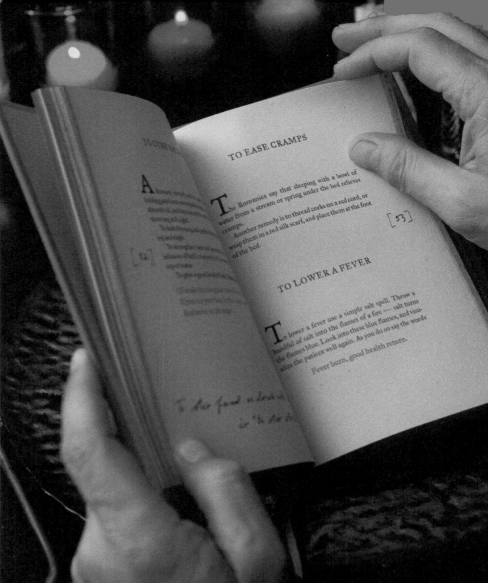

TO EASE CRAMPS

The Romanies say that sleeping with a bowl of water from a stream or spring under the bed relieves cramps.

Another remedy is to thread corks on a red cord, or wrap them in a red silk scarf, and place them at the foot of the bed.

[53]

TO LOWER A FEVER

To lower a fever use a simple salt spell. Throw a handful of salt into the flames of a fire — salt turns the flames blue. Look into these blue flames, and visualize the patient well again. As you do so say the words

Fever burn, good health return.

Menu

Preview
Drunken Heirloom Tomatoes
baby heirloom tomatoes first dipped in sherry
followed by a spice of chili or zatar

Spanish Goat Cheese Nachos

Begin
Touch of Tapas
Blonde gazpacho

Eggplant with manchego chorizo ragu

Paella cake grilled shrimp

Main
Spanish Style Chicken Paillard
napoleon of chicken layered with
snow peas, peppers, roasted garlic
layered potatoes
skewer of spanish olive, prosciutto and green tomato

Indulge
Caramelized Peach Rice Pudding
rice pudding served with caramelized peach and
peach ribbon paper tied with blanched chive

Libation
Sparkling Sangria
Spanish sparkling wine with
red berries and tarragon sprig garnish

Drunken Tomatoes with Chili Salt and Zatar Spice

Makes 10 servings

2 8-ounce baskets of small heirloom tomatoes

1 750ml bottle Spanish fino sherry

To serve, place the tomatoes in a bowl or platter accompanied by a small bowl of toothpicks (we use bamboo picks for a great look). In smaller bowls, serve the sherry, Chili Salt and Zatar Spice. Let guests know to take a tomato, dip it in the sherry and then in one of the spices.

Chili Salt
½ cup chili powder

2½ teaspoons cayenne powder

3 tablespoons kosher salt

Gently mix all ingredients and store in a tightly sealed container at room temperature.

Zatar Spice
4 tablespoons sesame seeds

3 tablespoons fresh picked thyme, ground fine

2 teaspoons kosher salt

1 tablespoon ground sumac

Toast sesame seeds in a dry skillet, cool and grind. Place in a bowl, add ground thyme, salt and sumac, mix well. Keep refrigerated until ready to use.

Spanish Goat Cheese Nachos

Makes 20 nachos

11 ounces goat cheese, log shaped

½ cup cornmeal

½ cup butter, garlic, olive oil mixture *(see recipe index)*

2 12-inch flour tortillas, cut into 20 2-inch medallions

2 cups Spanish port wine

3 tablespoons granulated sugar

1½ cups red grapes, cut into quarters

½ cup brown sugar, packed

4 tablespoons butter

1 bunch cilantro

With a cheese wire, slice the goat cheese into ⅛-inch medallions. Coat the slices in cornmeal and place on a tray to freeze for approximately 15 minutes until firm to the touch.

Meanwhile, dip tortilla circles in the butter garlic olive oil mixture, place on a baking sheet and bake in a 300 degree oven for 10 to 15 minutes until golden brown. Remove and set aside to cool.

In a saucepan, heat port wine and granulated sugar to a boil. Continue to boil until the mixture reduces to a syrup consistency.

In a non-stick pan over medium heat, sauté the goat cheese medallions in 2 tablespoons of butter until lightly browned and slightly softened. Keep a watchful eye on the cheese as it will melt and will not be usable if left in the pan too long. Remove from pan and place on the tortilla circles.

In the same non-stick pan, heat brown sugar and remaining 2 tablespoons of butter until the sugar starts to dissolve and becomes a golden color. Add the grapes and sauté until the color deepens and the grapes plump. Remove the pan from the heat and spoon a tablespoon of the mixture over each nacho. Drizzle with the port wine syrup, garnish with a small cilantro sprig and serve warm.

Touch of Tapas

Blonde Gazpacho
Makes 4 cups

1 pound yellow tomatoes, chopped

2 pounds yellow tomatoes for juicing

4 ounces English cucumber, chopped

2 ounces yellow bell pepper, chopped

1 ounce red onions, peeled and chopped

1 ounce celery, trimmed and chopped

1 teaspoon garlic, minced

2 tablespoons olive oil

1½ tablespoons red wine vinegar

Salt and pepper to taste

⅓ cup butter, garlic, olive oil mixture *(see recipe index)*

3 slices of white bread

1 bunch cilantro

To make the tomato juice, juice two pounds of yellow tomatoes.

Mix the chopped tomatoes, tomato juice, vegetables and garlic in a food processor and puree until smooth. You can do this in batches and mix in a bowl or container. This can be a little chunky if you like. Season with the olive oil, red wine vinegar, salt and pepper. Soup is best when prepared one day in advance and placed in the refrigerator to allow flavors to develop. Prior to serving, taste the soup and adjust the olive oil and vinegar if needed.

To prepare the croutons, cut the bread into spoon shapes with a cookie cutter or 3x½-inch sticks. Meanwhile warm a ½ cup of the butter, garlic, olive oil mixture in a sauté pan. Dip one side of the bread shapes in the mixture to coat well and place on a baking sheet. Sprinkle with salt and pepper. Bake in a 300 degree oven for 10 to 15 minutes until golden brown.

To serve, pour soup into a glass or bowl (we used a tall shot glass) and garnish with the toasted bread spoon and fresh cilantro and serve.

Eggplant with Manchego Chorizo Ragu
Makes 10 rolls

2 eggplants
½ cup of beef chorizo
½ cup grated manchego cheese and slices to serve under the roll
2 tablespoons fresh mint, chiffonade
10 blanched chives
½ cup Vegetable Marinade *(see recipe index)*

Slice the eggplant on a mandoline, about ⅛-inch thick lengthwise. Brush Vegetable Marinade on both sides of the eggplant and refrigerate overnight.

Cook chorizo in a pan until all juices evaporate, place on a paper towel until cooled. Mix the chorizo with the grated manchego cheese and mint.

Grill the eggplant on both sides and season with salt and pepper on a griddle. Place on paper towel to cool.

To assemble, place one tablespoon of the chorizo manchego filling on the eggplant and roll. Tie it together with a blanched chive and serve over a slice of manchego.

Paella Cake Grilled Shrimp

Makes 10 2-inch paella squares

10 medium shrimp (size 21/25), peeled, deveined and butterflied

1 cup chicken stock

¾ tablespoons clam base *(a paste available at specialty stores)*

Pinch of saffron threads

3 tablespoons butter

¼ cup onion, minced

2 teaspoons minced garlic

¼ cup red bell pepper, peeled and finely diced

¼ cup zucchini, finely diced

4 ounces Spanish sausages (we use hickory smoked pork that is fully cooked) finely diced

¼ cup Arborio rice

½ cup dry white wine

1 plum tomato, peeled and pureed

2 tablespoons grated parmesan

1 large beaten egg

Salt and pepper to taste

Vegetable oil to sauté the cakes

3 sprigs of fresh tarragon

Chimichurri Sauce *(see recipe index)*

Clean, peel and devein the shrimp then lightly butterfly the end. Toss in a ½ cup of Chimichurri Sauce. Place in a container and refrigerate overnight to marinate.

Bring chicken stock, clam base and saffron to a boil, reduce to low heat and let simmer.

In another pan, sauté the onions and garlic with butter until they are almost translucent. Then add the bell pepper, zucchini and sausage and cook until soft. Add the rice and stir to make sure it is coated with butter, and then add white wine. Cook, stirring constantly, until the liquid has almost completely evaporated. Stir in the pureed tomato then begin adding the simmering stock, about one quarter cup at a time, stirring continuously and making sure the rice has absorbed the stock before adding the next quarter cup. Repeat until the cup of chicken stock is absorbed.

Remove the pot from heat, stir in parmesan cheese and beaten egg. Immediately transfer the rice to a baking sheet that is lined with parchment paper and then sprayed with nonstick spray. Spread evenly in a 1¼-inch thick layer. Cover it with plastic wrap, smoothing it out with your hands to make sure the top is as even as possible. Refrigerate for two hours until the rice sets. You can store the rice this way up to 24 hours.

Cut the chilled paella into 10 2-inch square cakes. Sauté the paella cakes in vegetable oil, in batches, until golden brown on both sides. As the cakes are done, place them on a plate lined with paper towels to drain. Add a little more vegetable oil to the pan and sear the shrimp, about 2 minutes on each side, and transfer to a bowl. Add a ½ cup of Chimichurri sauce with the shrimp and toss lightly. Transfer the shrimp onto a baking sheet and bake in a 350 degree oven for 5 minutes. To assemble, place a small dollop of Chimichurri sauce in the center of a paella cake, then place one shrimp on the square, garnish with fresh tarragon and serve.

Spanish Style Chicken Paillard
Makes 10 servings

8 8-ounce chicken breasts, cut and pounded into 40 very thin medallions

Salt and pepper to taste

4 teaspoons garlic, minced

1 cup all-purpose flour

8 tablespoons butter

8 tablespoons olive oil

4 tablespoons Spanish smoked paprika

1 cup Spanish sherry

4 cups chicken broth, warmed

½ cup lemon juice

½ cup roasted garlic

3 each red and orange bell peppers

½ pound mange tout (snow peas)

10 cherry heirloom tomatoes

10 slices of prosciutto

10 Spanish queen size green olives

Fresh sage and yellow sweet pea sprouts for garnish

Layered Potatoes *(see recipe index)*

Cut the chicken breast into approximately 2-inch chunks and pound them out into medallions. Put the flour on a plate and sprinkle with salt and pepper. Then coat the pounded chicken medallions lightly in the flour. In a hot sauté pan, melt 1 tablespoon of butter and olive oil and place the chicken pieces in the pan, filling the entire pan surface with the chicken.

Sprinkle with more salt and pepper and add a little minced garlic. When one side of the chicken is brown, turn over to the other side and sprinkle with smoked paprika. When both sides are brown add the Spanish sherry to deglaze the pan and then add warm chicken broth. Next, add whole pieces of roasted garlic and lemon juice. Reduce the liquid a little so it thickens. Remove the chicken and place on a plate, drizzle the sauce from the pan over the chicken. Cut orange and red pepper in fat julienne pieces and grill, season with salt and pepper. Sauté the mange tout in a sauté pan with butter, salt and pepper. Then add the peppers and mange tout to the plate. Take a skewer (I use a metal one) and slide on an heirloom tomato, then weave on one slice of prosciutto and then place a green olive at the end and use as a garnish to the plate.

Caramelized Peach Rice Pudding

Makes 10 servings

Rice Pudding
Makes 10 3x3-inch squares

10 ounces long grain rice

4 cups boiling water

5 cups milk

1 cup heavy cream

1 tablespoon ground cinnamon

1 cup + 2 tablespoons granulated sugar

6 gelatin sheets

1 cup whipped cream

Cook rice and water for approximately 20 minutes or until rice is tender. Add 4½ cups milk, reserving ½ cup for dissolving the gelatin. Add heavy cream, cinnamon and sugar to tender rice and cook occasionally stirring the rice until all liquid is absorbed.

Dissolve gelatin sheets in ½ cup milk then add to the rice mixture. Fold in the whipped cream. Pour rice filling into a baking sheet lined with parchment paper and sprayed with non-stick spray. The rice pudding will only cover ¾ of the sheet. Chill for about 2 hours.

Caramelized Peaches

2 peaches, cut into ¼-inch slices

2 cups brown sugar

4 tablespoons butter

Melt brown sugar and butter on low heat until the sugar dissolves and turn up to medium heat until you have rolling bubbles. Add peach slices and cook until soft and brown color. Remove from heat and cool.

Peach Paper
Makes 1 baking sheet

1 cup (about 5 ounces) peaches

4 tablespoons granulated sugar

2 tablespoons plus 2 teaspoons water

2 teaspoons cornstarch

10 fresh chives, blanched

Preheat the oven to 250 degrees. Line a baking sheet with parchment paper and spray with non-stick spray.

In a medium saucepan, combine the chopped peaches, sugar and 2 tablespoons of water over medium heat. Cook for 3 to 4 minutes, or until the sugar dissolves and the water comes to a boil.

While the peaches are heating, in a small bowl, stir together 2 teaspoons water and cornstarch to form a slurry and stir constantly for 1 to 2 minutes. When the peaches reach a boil, add the slurry and stir constantly for 1 to 2 minutes or until the mixture comes to a rapid boil.

Remove the pan from the heat and let cool to room temperature.

Transfer the cooled mixture to a food processor and purée until smooth.

Spread the peach purée on the prepared sheet. Form as thin a layer as you can. Holes may or may not form as the paper dries.

Bake for 10 minutes, and then turn the oven off and leave for about 6 hours or overnight. Wrap with plastic wrap and store at room temperature.

Assembling the dessert:

Cut chilled Rice Pudding into 10 3x3-inch squares. Place a square of pudding on the plate and lean a peach slice on it. Tear the peach paper into 3-inch strips and tie across the middle with a blanched chive to create a fan. Place the fan on the peach slice and serve.

Sparkling Sangria

1 bottle Spanish sparkling wine

1 cup each sliced red apples, sliced strawberries, red raspberries

Several blackberries and/or blueberries

Sprig of tarragon

1 cup puree of strawberries

Pour sparkling wine in a pitcher, add puree of strawberries and mix in all fruit and a sprig of tarragon. Pour into each glass, add tarragon for garnish.

Playing With Color

At a dinner party, the center of the world becomes the table. For a couple of hours, you and your friends are focused on each other and that world. Why not make it the most beautiful world possible? One way to do this is to simply theme the design around one color. For this party, I was inspired by the color red. As a high energy color, I believe it actually helps bring on conversation.

Different shades of the same color can be used in the napkins, flowers, china and glassware to create a look that has "texture." And, yes, I also used red wine glasses. I know that some purists believe wine should only be served in clear glasses, but I feel it's okay to mix it up a bit. However, if you prefer clear wine glasses, then use them and add colored water glasses to the table instead.

Seating Charts

For small dinner parties I like to assign seating using something creative that goes with my theme. In this case, the books were my place cards. To add this extra touch, look at your menu and your inspiration for having the party itself. For a fall party, perhaps a leaf with each name written on it and placed in the center of the plate would be perfect. For a beach theme, driftwood can be used as the place card with a paper card inserted in it. Even a shell can become a place card. The possibilities are endless and you can't go wrong – everyone will appreciate the extra time you spent and the personalized touch it gives the party.

FUEL
The passion that drives us

This party was inspired by Liese Gardner, a dear friend and owner of Mecca Communications, who does some truly inspiring work for the special events and catering industries. Liese wanted to bring 100 like-minded individuals from our industry together to share with one another what drives their passion outside of the work place.

The kitchen of Good Gracious! made the perfect venue for this event. But throwing a party in your "home" always makes you see it with new eyes and there were still some little things we wanted to do to really make our kitchen shine.

Because we are a city location, we don't have tons of space, but we do have a small, enclosed area outside our kitchen. We turned this into a hip, contemporary city patio for the evening by placing eight-foot tall ficus hedge boxes around the perimeter, carpeting over the asphalt and bringing in some very groovy lounge furniture. We dimmed the lights inside instead of using our oh-so-practical fluorescent lighting and each work station was shining in all its stainless-steel glory.

Because the theme of the event was what "fuels" us, guests were asked beforehand to bring art, guitars, drums…whatever drives their passions. Entertainment ranged from gospel songs to Mexican folklore music - as eclectic as the menu we created. We served homey food that was easy to eat and, in the case of the panna cotta, actually followed the color palette of the invitation! We used napkins and rented glass plates that also fell within the event's color theme.

The details of this event were exciting to us and it was fun to bring people into our "home" for a very intimate, special event. We didn't have to bring any art or instruments because truly, what fuels us here at Good Gracious! is our passion for food and design and how it makes people feel at the time, and how they fondly remember the moment in the future.

Menu

Inspired Chips
Lemon Thyme Parsnip

Taro Smoky Coriander

Lotus Root Ginger Garlic

Beetroot Sea Salt

Potato Rosemary

Plantain Spring Onion

Eggplant Parmesan

Inspired Dips
Blue Cheese Ricotta Feta Walnut

Yellow Beet Chimichurri

Curried Hummus

Herbed Lima Bean

Green Tomato Cilantro

Spiced Yogurt

Inspired Savory Panna Cotta Cakes
Curried Cauliflower Leek

Carrot Ginger thyme

Broccoli and Mushroom

Inspired Pies
Savory Beef Stroganoff, Chicken Curry and Lamb
Caponata pastry pies dusted with flavored salts

Inspired Summer Soups
Chilled BLT: Bacon, Lettuce and Tomato

Cucumber, Yogurt and Dill

Libation
Sparkling Prosecco
served with a fresh rosemary wand
and blueberries

INSPIRED CHIPS

Each vegetable provides 10–20 slices of chips, depending on its size. For buffet style service, we prepare about 6 chips per guest.

Lemon Thyme Parsnip Chips

Peel and slice parsnips in paper thin slices lengthways then place into hot oil to fry. For the lemon thyme salt, mix some lemon zest and thyme stems in the salt a couple days before and let it sit. When it is time to use the salt, just remove the stems and add in some chopped thyme. After the parsnip chips are fried, sprinkle with the lemon thyme salt.

Taro Smoky Coriander Chips

Peel and slice taro in paper thin slices diagonally, then place into hot oil to fry. For the smoked coriander salt, toss whole coriander seeds in liquid smoke and then bake in the oven for 5 to 7 minutes at 325 degrees. Remove from the oven, drain out any liquid, cool the seeds and grind. Mix with the salt until desired flavor is reached.

Lotus Root Ginger Garlic Chips

It is best to use the lotus root that is packaged, peeled and soaked in water. Slice the root in paper thin slices then place into hot oil to fry. Remove from the oil and sprinkle with powdered ginger and powdered garlic. Hint: You can stain lotus root in food colored water for about 1 day before you slice them if you want to have a unique colored chip.

Beetroot Sea Salt Chips

Par cook the beets by placing them in boiling water for 5 minutes, then remove. When cool enough to handle, peel the beets and then slice into paper thin slices. Place into hot oil to fry. Remove from the oil and sprinkle with sea salt.

Plantain Spring Onion Chips

Peel and slice plantains in paper thin slices lengthwise and then place into hot oil to fry. Sprinkle with finely chopped scallions, onion powder, salt and pepper.

Potato Rosemary Chips

Peel potato and slice into paper thin slices, then place into hot oil to fry.

For the rosemary salt, mix rosemary stems into salt for a couple of days and let sit. When it comes time to use the salt, just remove the stems and add chopped rosemary. Sprinkle onto the fried potato chips.

Eggplant Parmesan Chips

Slice baby eggplants in half lengthways and then cut them into three or four spears. Lightly toss with olive oil and bake in the oven for 25 to 30 minutes at 350 degrees until crispy. Sprinkle with parmesan cheese and serve.

BLUE CHEESE RICOTTA FETA WALNUT DIP

Makes 2 cups

1 teaspoon roasted garlic

1 cup walnut halves, toasted

¾ cup feta cheese, crumbled

¾ cup ricotta

3 tablespoons stilton cheese

½ cup milk

1 teaspoon dried oregano

¼ cup flat-leaf parsley

Freshly ground black pepper

½ teaspoon crushed red pepper flakes

1 tablespoon olive oil

Combine all the ingredients except olive oil in a food processor and pulse until smooth.

Place in a serving bowl and drizzle with olive oil.

YELLOW BEET CHIMICHURRI DIP

Makes 3 cups

1½ pounds yellow beets

2 tablespoons pickled ginger (with juice)

½ tablespoon minced garlic

½ serrano chile, roasted peeled and seeded

2 tablespoons yellow miso paste

2 tablespoons lemon juice

¼ cup olive oil

Salt and black pepper

Roast the beets in the oven until tender. When cool enough to handle, peel the beets and cut into pieces to place into the food processor. Put all the ingredients, except for the olive oil, into the food processor and pulse until smooth. Add the olive oil slowly until it is emulsified. Season with salt and pepper to taste. The flavor should be sharp and lemony. This can only be made the same day it is used.

CURRY HUMMUS DIP

Makes 2 cups

1½ cups drained canned garbanzo beans

3 tablespoons water

⅓ cup tahini

1 teaspoon salt

¼ teaspoon ground cumin

3 tablespoons lemon juice

½ tablespoon minced garlic

2 tablespoons extra virgin olive oil

1 pinch cayenne

2 pinches black pepper

1 tablespoon curry paste

Place all the ingredients into a food processor and blend until smooth. If necessary, add a little more lemon juice or water to thin to your desired consistency.

HERBED LIMA BEAM DIP

Makes 2 cups

10 ounces of frozen baby lima beans (defrosted)

2 tablespoons chopped fresh cilantro

2 tablespoons chopped fresh flat-leaf parsley

1 tablespoon chopped fresh dill

1 tablespoon chopped fresh mint

½ teaspoon ground cumin

⅛ teaspoon cayenne pepper, or to taste

2 tablespoons fresh lemon juice

3 tablespoons extra virgin olive oil

Place all the ingredients into a food processor and blend until smooth. Add salt and pepper to taste.

GREEN TOMATO CILANTRO SALSA

Makes 4 cups

1¼ pounds tomatillos, husked and washed

1¼ pounds green tomatoes

1 cup finely chopped green onion

¾ cup cilantro, chopped

2 roasted jalapenos, peeled and seeded

1½ tablespoons minced garlic

Salt and pepper to taste

Roast tomatillos and green tomatoes in a dry sauté pan over medium heat until they are charred and soft. Let them cool.

Place all the ingredients into a food processor and blend until smooth. Add salt and pepper to taste.

SPICED YOGURT DIP

Make 2 cups

2 cups nonfat yogurt

⅛ cup lemon juice

⅛ cup chopped mint

Pinch ground cumin

Pinch ground coriander

Pinch ground chill powder

Zest of 1 lime

Salt and pepper

Mix together in a small bowl. Add salt and pepper to taste.

SAVORY PANNA COTTA

Each recipe makes 3 cups of mixture. Suggested serving size 2 tablespoons per individual container

Carrot Ginger

5 sheets gelatin *(available in specialty stores)*

⅛ cup milk

2 cups heavy cream

1 sprig fresh thyme

1 tablespoon grated ginger

3 cups chicken broth

2 carrots, chopped

4 thick carrots for the base

4 carrots sliced very thin lengthwise on the mandoline for garnish

Soak the gelatin in the milk and ½ cup cream until softened, then take the rest of the cream, thyme and ginger and bring it to a boil in a pot. Remove the thyme stems and add to the gelatin mixture and stir until dissolved.

Simmer the 2 chopped carrots in another pot with the chicken broth until soft. Strain the carrots, reserving broth for later use, and purée. Add puréed carrots to the gelatin cream mixture. Pour the liquid mixture into individual molds and chill for 4 hours. Hint: we freeze the molds to ensure easy removal and then let the frozen panna cotta come to room temperature.

Meanwhile, take the carrots for the base and slice into ⅛-inch thick disks and simmer in the reserved chicken broth until just past al dente stage. Remove and strain, saving the chicken broth again. Chill the carrot disks and reserve.

Take the remaining carrots and slice on the mandoline into 2-inch long pieces. Add the carrot slices to the remaining chicken broth and simmer until al dente. Remove from the broth and strain. Place in a bowl and toss in the chopped thyme and kosher salt. Place this in the refrigerator to chill.

To assemble, unmold the panna cottas onto the carrot disks, mold carrot curls onto the top and serve.

Broccoli and Mushroom

5 sheets of gelatin *(available in specialty stores)*
⅛ cup milk
2 cups heavy cream
3 cups chicken broth
6 ounces broccoli florets
2 cups shiitake mushrooms cut in small dice
2 tablespoons butter
½ tablespoon roasted garlic
Salt and pepper
Mushroom Duxelle topping *(recipe to follow)*
1 English cucumber

Soak gelatin in the milk and ½ cup cream until softened. Take the rest of the cream and bring to a boil in a pot. Add the gelatin mixture to the boiling cream and stir until dissolved.

Simmer the broccoli in a separate pot with the chicken broth until soft. Strain the broccoli and purée. Add to the gelatin cream mixture.

In a sauté pan, sauté the mushrooms with butter and cook until golden brown. Add the roasted garlic, salt and pepper. Add this mushroom mixture to the cream mixture. Pour the liquid into individual molds and chill for 4 hours. Hint: we freeze the molds to ensure easy removal and then let the frozen panna cotta come to room temperature.

Meanwhile, cut the cucumber into ⅛-inch slices and set aside.

To assemble, unmold the panna cottas onto the cucumber slices. Top with a teaspoon of Mushroom Duxelle and serve.

Mushroom Duxelle
Makes 2 cups

1½ pounds shiitake mushrooms, diced
½ pound shallots, finely diced
1 tablespoon minced garlic
1 tablespoon fresh chopped rosemary
1 tablespoon fresh chopped thyme
1 tablespoon fresh chopped parsley
2 tablespoons butter
2 tablespoons olive oil
Salt and pepper to taste
1 cup of wine, port, Madeira or sherry

Mix the mushrooms, shallots, garlic, herbs, butter and olive oil together and sauté over high heat until all the liquid evaporates and mixture is light brown. Add the wine, adjust seasonings to taste and continue to sauté until the liquid evaporates.

Curry Cauliflower Leek

5 gelatin sheets *(available in specialty stores)*
⅛ cup milk
2 cups heavy cream
3 cups chicken broth
6 ounces cauliflower florets
1½ tablespoons curry paste *(available in grocery stores)*
1 cup raw leeks, small dice + 3 cups julienne leeks for topping
1 tablespoon butter
1 teaspoon roasted garlic
Salt and pepper to taste
½ teaspoon yellow gold food dye
1 ounce tarragon
2 cups Shortcrust Pastry Mix *(see recipe index)*
Egg Wash to brush the disks

Soak the gelatin in the milk and ½ cup cream until softened, then take the rest of the cream and bring it to a boil in a pot. Add the gelatin mixture to the boiling cream and stir until dissolved.

Simmer the cauliflower in another pot with chicken broth and 1 tablespoon curry paste until soft, then strain and purée. Sauté the diced leeks with butter, ½ tablespoon curry paste, roasted garlic, salt and pepper. Add the cauliflower and the diced leeks to the cream mixture and stir in the yellow food coloring.

Pour the liquid mixture into individual molds and chill for 4 hours. Hint: we freeze the molds to ensure easy removal and then let the frozen panna cotta come to room temperature.

Meanwhile, fry the julienne leeks and tarragon until crispy and set aside.

Mix the Shortcrust Pastry Mix with ¼ cup water and mold to a soft dough. Roll the dough out with some flour until you get a ⅛-inch thickness. Cut out into 2-inch circles. Brush with Egg Wash and bake in a 325 degree oven for 10 minutes until light and golden. Push down on the disks if they puff up.

To assemble, unmold the panna cottas onto the short crust disks and then garnish with the crispy leeks and tarragon mixture.

BEEF STROGANOFF PIES

Makes 25 pies

2 pounds beef tenderloin, small diced

½ cup olive oil

Salt and pepper

¼ cup butter

¼ cup all-purpose flour

1½ cups beef stock

3½ cups onions, thinly sliced

1½ tablespoons sour cream

1 teaspoon Dijon mustard

3½ cups mushrooms, cut into quarters

¼ cup brandy

4 cups Shortcrust Pastry Mix *(see recipe index)*

½ cup water

½ teaspoon onion powder

Egg Wash *(see recipe index)*

Melted butter

2 teaspoons grey sea salt mixed with 2 teaspoons herbs de Provence, equal parts

Season beef with salt and pepper. Melt 2 tablespoons of butter in a large sauce pan over medium-high heat, add onions and mushrooms and sauté approximately 10 minutes until golden brown. Put aside and save any juices.

Melt 2 tablespoons more butter in same pan on high heat and add the beef, cook quickly, shaking the pan and stirring until evenly browned, approximately 1 to 2 minutes. The meat should remain pink in the center. Remove the meat from the pan and save the juices. Deglaze the pan with brandy.

Add 2 tablespoons more of butter with the flour to make a roux, add the juices back to the pan with the beef stock. Bring to a boil and then reduce heat to a simmer. When the sauce has slightly thickened, add sour cream and mustard. Do not let this boil. Check seasoning and add salt and pepper to taste. When sauce is at the right constituency add back to the mushrooms, onions and beef.

Mix the Shortcrust Pastry Mix with ½ cup of water and ½ teaspoon onion powder to form a dough. Roll out the dough to ⅛-inch thickness and cut into 3x3-inch squares. Place squares into greased muffin tins and fill with beef stroganoff to the top. Fold the dough edges over the mixture and turn the corners back over to create a design. Brush with Egg Wash, melted butter and sprinkle with grey sea salt mixture. Bake in the oven at 375 degrees until golden brown, about 20 to 30 minutes. Note: These can be frozen until ready to cook.

CHICKEN CURRY PIES
Makes 25 pies

¾ pounds chicken breast, diced

1 cup Vegetable Marinade
(see recipe index)

1 tablespoon + 1½ cups curry paste

1 tablespoon + ¼ cup minced garlic

Salt and pepper

¼ cup butter, garlic, olive oil mixture
(see recipe index)

4 cups yellow onions, diced

2 cups carrots, diced

2 cups celery, diced

4 cups cauliflower (1 head), diced

4 cups bell peppers (mix colors), diced

4 cups zucchini (green and yellow), diced

2 cups mushrooms, diced

1¼ cups mild curry paste

14 ounces of whipped cream cheese, room
temperature

4 cups Shortcrust Pastry Mix
(see recipe index)

½ cup water

½ teaspoon onion powder

Egg Wash *(see recipe index)*

Melted butter

Curry Salt topping
Makes 1 cup

5 tablespoons curry powder

3 tablespoons grey sea salt

1 tablespoon paprika

1 tablespoon white pepper

Marinate the chicken the day before in the Vegetable Marinade and 1 tablespoon curry paste. Next day, sauté the chicken with 1 tablespoon garlic, ¼ cup curry paste, salt and pepper. Do not overcook the chicken. When the chicken is done, set aside.

Cut all vegetables into a small dice. Sauté vegetables and ¼ cup garlic in a pan with the butter, garlic, olive oil mixture until soft. Add 1¼ cup curry paste cook over medium heat. Stir frequently until all water is cooked out. Season with salt and pepper. Fold curry chicken into the vegetables, mixing well. In a mixing bowl, beat the cream cheese until light and fluffy, then fold into vegetable chicken mixture.

Mix the Shortcrust Pastry Mix with ½ cup of water and ½ teaspoon onion powder to form a dough. Roll out the dough to ⅛-inch thickness and cut into 3½-inch circles. Place circles on a flat surface and brush with Egg Wash. Place a spoonful of the chicken filling in the middle. Fold the pie outer edges together in the middle and pinch the edges of the dough together. Brush with melted butter. Sprinkle heavily with the curry salt topping. Bake in the oven at 375 degrees 20 to 30 minutes until golden brown and cooked.
Note: These can be frozen until ready to cook.

LAMB CAPONATA PIES
Makes 25 pies

Lamb filling

1 tablespoon vegetable oil

2½ pounds ground lamb

5 cups of Eggplant Caponata *(recipe to follow)*

⅓ cup chopped mint

2 tablespoons chopped parsley

2 tablespoons chopped chives

1 tablespoon lemon juice

Salt and pepper

2 tablespoons garlic

4 cups Shortcrust Pastry Mix *(see recipe index)*

½ cup water

½ teaspoon onion powder

Egg Wash *(see recipe index)*

Melted butter

Salt topping
Makes 1 cup

3 tablespoons black pepper

5 tablespoons poppyseeds

3 tablespoons grey sea salt

Brown the lamb with garlic in a heavy pot and season with salt and pepper. Remove from the heat and allow to cool. Add the Eggplant Caponata to the lamb and mix together with the herbs and lemon juice.

Combine the Shortcrust Pastry Mix with a ½ cup of water and a ½ teaspoon onion powder to form a dough. Roll out the dough to a ⅛-inch thickness and cut into 3¼-inch circles. Place the circles on a flat surface and brush with Egg Wash. Place a spoonful of the lamb filling in the middle. Fold the dough over to create a half moon shape and seal the edges together with a fork. Brush with melted butter. Sprinkle heavily with the salt topping.

Bake in the oven at 375 degrees for 20 to 30 minutes until golden brown. Note: These can be frozen until ready to cook.

Eggplant Caponata
Makes 5 cups

3 regular eggplants

¼ cup olive oil

3 cups diced tomatoes (canned)

¼ cup minced garlic

2 cups tomato juice

1 tablespoon chopped rosemary

1 tablespoon chopped thyme

½ tablespoon ground black pepper

1 tablespoon salt.

Slice eggplant into ½-inch thick slices, sprinkle with salt and let rest for 20 minutes. Squeeze the water out of the eggplant using paper towels. Dice the eggplant. Add olive oil to a sauté pan and sauté the garlic until soft. Add the eggplant and remainder of the ingredients, cover and cook over a low heat for approximately 3 hours until the mixture is reduced and thick.

CHILLED BLT SOUP

Makes 4 cups

⅓ cup shallots

⅓ cup white onions

1 teaspoon garlic

3 slices bacon chopped + 3 slices of bacon to make bits for topping

1½ cups fresh tomatoes cut into medium cubes

1½ cups canned tomatoes

⅔ cup beef broth

1 cup chicken broth

⅔ cup tomato juice

1 tablespoon tomato paste

Salt and pepper

½ head of romaine, shredded small and fine

1 cup olive oil for garnish

2 teaspoons granulated sugar

In a heavy-duty pot sauté the bacon on high heat until cooked and golden brown. Add the onions, shallots and garlic and cook until translucent and brown. Add tomatoes and cook until the mixture reduces and becomes thicker.

Add the beef and chicken broths, tomato juice and tomato paste. Bring to a boil then reduce heat and simmer for 20 minutes. Remove from the heat and let cool slightly. When cool enough to handle, place the mixture into a processor or blender to purée. Check seasonings and add a little sugar if needed.

Meanwhile, lay the remaining 3 slices of bacon on a sheet pan and bake in a 350 degree oven for 10 to 15 minutes or until crispy. Strain all the fat off and place bacon on paper towels. When cool, crumble the bacon.

Serve the soup in demitasse cups with bacon bits sprinkled on top. Garnish with shredded romaine lettuce and drizzle with olive oil.

CUCUMBER YOGURT DILL SOUP

Makes 4 cups

1 English cucumber, peeled seeded and coarsely chopped

3 tablespoons fresh chopped mint

2 large scallions

1½ tablespoons chopped fresh dill

1 clove garlic, crushed

2 cups low fat or nonfat yogurt

Salt and ground white pepper

Garnish: cucumber wands

In a food processor or blender, purée the cucumber, mint, scallions, dill and garlic until well combined but not smooth. Add yogurt and continue to purée until smooth. Chill for 4 to 6 hours or overnight. Adjust seasonings and serve the soup in a demitasse cup garnished with a cucumber wand.

There are rental companies all over the country that have a wonderful range of products that can give your party the look that is right for you. Research the best in your area and when you visit them, ask to see what styles of china, glassware, flatware and linen they carry. Many rental companies have planners on staff who will work with you to put together a color scheme for your tabletop and some will even do basic lighting to help add a professional and cost effective look to your event. Remember, the best thing about renting equipment is that you won't have to do dishes or laundry after the party!

In the case of this event, we rented the box hedges that were so instrumental in turning the look of our back patio into such a chic space. We've rented artwork, antiques, carpet and more for parties. When it comes to rentals, we can find almost anything!

Thyme in a bottle

Don't be afraid to explore uses for herbs other than food. Herbs also go very well with beverages. Here, we've used rosemary stems to add an unusual yet very pleasing essence to a typical Prosecco drink, thereby making it a little more exotic. You can also use skewers with basil or sage leaves woven on them to place in a beverage. Don't be afraid to experiment! Don't worry if you want that basil drink in the middle of winter – by freezing seasonal herbs in individual bags you can enjoy these fresh flavors throughout the year.

LADIES WHO DO TEA
An afternoon tradition

❝ *There are few hours in life more agreeable than the hour dedicated to the ceremony known as afternoon tea."*
– Anonymous

Visit any household in England and the first thing you will be offered is a nice cup of tea. Of course, being English myself, I was raised on the notion that a nice cup of tea can put anything – small or large – to rights. Sadly, the tradition of afternoon tea has somewhat died and is now reserved for special occasions.

It was such an occasion that Annette, the mother of Dan Smith, a Senior Event Planner with Good Gracious!, wanted to create for her very good friends; the women in the Assistance League Organization she has known for more than 30 years. Normally they hold an annual Afternoon Tea at a hotel, but Annette wanted a more intimate gathering at her home. In getting to know her, I discovered Annette was a collector of depression glass. There could be no lovelier way to display and serve this menu than with this precious collection!

The guests gathered at three o'clock. As classical music filled the room, each woman was given a wrist corsage to make her feel special. With a glass of sherry in hand and good conversation, the afternoon soon became very intimate and relaxed. I served an interpretation of afternoon tea foods that brought together my heritage and my contemporary tastes. As a guest, I sat with the ladies as we shared these delicacies as well as stories, recipes, tea and laughter. Needless to say the taste of friendship and tea lingered as we packaged a variety of foods to take home with us. As I think about it now, perhaps it isn't the tea that cures all the ills of the English; it's obviously the friendships forged over those of cups of hot, sweet tea.

Menu

Dainty Sandwiches
English cucumber watercress over sweet butter
with a touch of celery walnut crumb

Smoked salmon dill with lemon caper butter

Roast beef spring onions with horseradish cream

Lightly curried chicken with mango chutney

Cheddar cheese with Branston pickle

Petite Heart Shaped Scones
fresh blueberry and candied lemon with poppy seed
served with clotted cream and lemon curd

Quail Scotch Eggs
quail eggs wrapped in crispy sausage

English Sweet Pea Country Ham Tartlet
doll house savory shortcrust pastry filled with a sweet
pea country ham cheese custard

Shortbread
Traditional shortbread

Caramelized walnut shortbread

Somerset Apple Cider Cake
apple cider soaked golden raisin cake
with vanilla glaze

Classic Victoria Sponge
sponge cake filled with a raspberry preserve
fresh whipped cream, dusted with powdered sugar

Bowl of Cherries
bowl of new season Queen Anne cherries

Trio of Sherry
oloroso, amontallado and fino

DAINTY TEA SANDWICHES

Lightly Curried Chicken with Mango Chutney

2 slices of curried coconut bread (or your choice of bread)

Curry chicken filling (recipe to follow)

2 tablespoons mango chutney puree (available at grocery stores, pureed to make smooth)

Curry Chicken filling

Makes filling for 16 whole sandwiches

¾ pounds chicken breast, diced

1 cup Vegetable Marinade (see recipe index)

1 cup curry paste

4 tablespoons minced garlic

Salt and pepper

3 tablespoons butter, garlic, olive oil mix (see recipe index)

2 cups yellow onions, diced

1 cup carrots, diced

1 cup celery, diced

2 cups cauliflower, diced

2 cups bell peppers (mix colors), diced

2 cups zucchini (green and yellow), diced

1 cup mushrooms, diced

7 ounces of whipped cream cheese, room temperature

Marinate chicken the day before with Vegetable Marinade and 1 tablespoon curry paste. The next day, sauté the chicken with 1 tablespoon of garlic, ¼ cup curry paste, salt and pepper. Do not over cook. When done, mince to a very small dice in a food processor and set aside.

Cut all the vegetables in a food processor until minced into very small pieces. Sauté in a pan with butter, garlic, olive oil mixture until soft. Add ⅔ cup of the curry paste and 3 tablespoons of garlic and cook over medium heat. Stir frequently until all the water is cooked out, season with salt and pepper. Fold the cooked chicken mixture into the vegetable curry, mixing well.

In a mixing bowl, beat the cream cheese until light and fluffy. Fold cream cheese into vegetable chicken mixture.

Cucumber Sandwich

2 slices of thinly sliced white bread

2 tablespoons butter/cream cheese mix (mix together 2/3 butter and 1/3 cream cheese with salt and pepper)

2 sprigs watercress

1 teaspoon chopped walnuts

1 teaspoon chopped celery

18 thin slices cucumber

Salt and white pepper.

Smoked Salmon Dill with Lemon Caper Butter
Served open faced

1 slice of thinly sliced pumpernickel bread cut out into 4 1¼ inch circles

2 tablespoons of lemon caper butter mix (mix butter with capers and lemon zest)

½ slice of smoked salmon

Dollop of lemon caper butter

Dill sprigs for garnish

Roast Beef Spring Onions with Horseradish Cream

2 slices of thinly sliced white bread

2 tablespoons of horseradish butter cream cheese mix (⅔ butter and ⅓ cream cheese with grated horseradish to taste)

Three slices of beef tenderloin seared, cooked and sliced

1 tablespoon caramelized spring onions (see recipe index)

Branston Pickle Cheddar Sandwich

2 slices of thinly sliced wheat bread

2 tablespoons Branston butter (mix Branston pickle with butter so you can taste the pickle)

2 thin slices cheddar cheese

Assemble the tea sandwiches:

Butter two slices of bread and spread with fillings to create the sandwiches. Trim off the crusts and cut into the shapes of your choice.

squares

triangles

fingers   circles

BLUEBERRY AND CANDIED LEMON WITH POPPYSEED SCONES

Makes 25 small scones

8 cups all-purpose flour

1¾ cups granulated sugar

2½ teaspoons baking powder

1½ teaspoons baking soda

1½ teaspoons salt

½ pound margarine cut in small pieces

1 cup milk

Mix all dry ingredients together by hand to a crumb consistency. This creates the scone "mix."

Take the scone mix and add about 1 cup of milk, mixing it together to make proper "biscuit consistency." Then pat the dough out on a floured flat service until about 1-inch thick. Cut into shapes with cutter or knife. Bake in a 325 degree oven for 7 to 10 minutes until lightly browned.

For blueberry scones, spread the dough out on a flat service until about ½-inch thick. Spread fresh blueberries on half of the dough and fold the other half over the blueberries and press together. Bake in a 325 degree oven for 7 to 10 minutes until lightly browned. When cooled, dust with powdered sugar.

For lemon poppyseed scones, add lemon zest and poppy seeds to the scone mix when adding the milk. Bake in a 350 degree oven for 7 to 10 minutes until lightly browned.

QUAIL SCOTCH EGG

Makes 8 scotch eggs

1 pound pork sausage (2 ounces of sausage per quail egg)

1 beaten egg

8 hard boiled quail eggs

1 cup of bread crumbs

Frying oil to fill a saucepan or a fryer

To cook a hard boiled quail egg perfectly: Place a pot of water on the stove over high heat with a sprinkle of salt. Wait for it to come to a rapid boil. Add the room temperature eggs slowly and carefully into the boiling water. When the water comes back to a boil, start timing for 7 minutes. When the time is up, pour out the hot water and flush the eggs with cold water until the eggs are cold. This process makes the eggs easy to peel and does not turn the eggs a grey color.

Mix the beaten egg into the sausage meat until smooth. Wrap the sausage meat around one of the peeled hard boiled eggs completely and evenly. Roll gently and evenly in the fresh breadcrumbs. Shake off any excess. Repeat with the rest of the eggs.

Heat oil in a saucepan or fryer to 275 degrees. Put wrapped eggs into the oil and fry until deep golden in color, about 8 minutes. When finished, place on a tray lined with a paper towel to drain. Cut in half or quarters and serve. Note: You can make Scotch Eggs with regular eggs as well.

ENGLISH SWEET PEA HAM TARTLET

Makes 25 small tartlets

1 cup heavy cream

3 egg yolks

4 ounces goat cheese, softened

2 tablespoons gruyere cheese, grated

2 tablespoons munster cheese, grated

2 tablespoons parmesan cheese, grated

½ teaspoon salt

½ teaspoon white pepper

½ cup country ham, cut into tiny cubes

½ cup sweet peas

2 tablespoons parsley, chopped

2 cups Shortcrust Pastry Mix *(see recipe index)*

Blend together the cream and egg yolks. Whisk in the goat cheese, then fold in all other cheeses, ham and peas. Season to taste with salt and white pepper, set aside.

To form the dough, take 2 cups of Shortcrust Pastry Mix and knead with ⅛ to ¼ cup water.

Roll out the Shortcrust Pastry dough to a ¼-inch thickness and cut out circles with a 3¼-inch cutter. Mold the circles into a tartlet mold. Place in the freezer until frozen so that the dough settles into the molds. When ready to prepare, remove the pastry molds from the freezer and place in a 300 degree oven and par-bake to half cooked for 6 to 7 minutes. Take out and push down any raised areas.

To assemble the tartlets. Spoon the mixture into the prepared tartlet shells and sprinkle with a little chopped parsley. Bake in a 275 degree oven for about 15 to 20 minutes so that the crust on the tartlet is cooked and the top is golden brown.

SHORTBREADS
Makes an 11x17-inch sheet pan

Plain shortbread base

6 cups all-purpose flour

1½ cups granulated sugar

1½ pounds cold butter, cut into small cubes

Walnut shortbread base

4 cups all-purpose flour

1 cup granulated sugar

1 pound cold butter, cut into small cubes

Topping for walnut shortbread

8 ounces unsalted butter

¾ cup dark corn syrup

½ cup dark brown sugar

4½ cups walnut pieces

For both bases:
Mix everything together in a bowl, crumbling lightly with your hands. Be sure that you don't push too hard with your fingers that it makes lumps. It should be light and flaky with all the butter incorporated. Spread the shortbread dough out evenly onto a sheet pan. You can cover it with plastic wrap and smooth it down with a metal spatula to make it smooth and compressed.

For Plain Shortbread:
Place shortbread in the oven at 325 degrees for about 15 minutes. It will be slightly golden and bounce back if you touch it. Remove from the oven and sprinkle lightly with granulated sugar while it is still hot, covering it completely. Let it cool.

For Walnut Shortbread:
Prepare the walnut shortbread in the same method as the plain shortbread. While baking, prepare the walnut topping by combining all ingredients except for the walnuts in a pot and melt it over a medium heat. When it comes to a boil, take off the heat and fold in the nuts. When the shortbread base is done baking, spread the nut topping evenly over the top, pushing the nuts into the shortbread. Drizzle the sauce all over the top to coat evenly. Bake in a 350 degree oven for 15 to 20 minutes until you get a rapid boil of the sugar in the nuts. Remove from the oven and let cool. Cut into desired shapes when cooled.

SOMERSET APPLE CIDER CAKE

Makes one 10-inch cake

Filling

1¼ pounds raisins

1½ cups apple cider

1½ pounds apples

1 pound sugar

12 ounces butter

4 eggs

1¼ pounds all-purpose flour

3 teaspoons baking powder

2 teaspoons allspice

Glaze for one cake

2 cups powdered sugar

½ teaspoon vanilla extract

4 tablespoons milk

Prepare a 10-inch baking pan by brushing with melted butter or spraying with non-stick spray and lining the bottom with parchment paper. Set aside. Next, bring apple cider to a boil in a medium pot. In a separate dish, place the raisins and then cover with the hot apple cider to allow raisins to plump.

Peel and core apples. Chop 1 pound of the apples and set aside for the cake. Set aside the remaining ½ pound of apples for garnish. Cream sugar and butter together in a kitchen mixer until light and fluffy. Beat the eggs separately and then add them gradually to the creamed mixture, beating well after each addition. Sift flour, baking powder and allspice together in a separate bowl, then add slowly to the creamed mixture. Add the chopped apples, raisins and any remaining cider.

Pour the mixture into a cake pan and bake in the oven at 350 degrees for 1 hour and 45 minutes. Test for doneness by pushing on the top of the cake with your finger. If it bounces back it is done. Remove from oven and cool.

Meanwhile, prepare the glaze. Whisk ingredients in a bowl until they become a liquid glaze that holds its shape when you pour. When cake is cool, pour the glaze over the cake and let set. Slice the ½ pound of apples, set aside earlier, to garnish the cake.

CLASSIC VICTORIA SPONGE
Makes a 10-inch cake

8 ounces unsalted butter

8 ounces granulated sugar

4 eggs beaten

2 teaspoons vanilla extract

8 ounces sifted cake flour

2 cups whipping cream

½ cup strawberry or raspberry jam

½ cup sifted powdered sugar

Cream butter and sugar together with a mixer until light and fluffy.

Add eggs, one at a time, along with vanilla, making sure they are fully incorporated each time.

Fold in the flour, being careful not to over mix.

Prepare 2 10-inch cake pans by lining with parchment paper then spraying with non-stick spray. Divide the cake batter evenly into the 2 pans. Bake in the oven at 350 degrees for 20 minutes or until the cake springs back when touched. Remove from the oven and cool.

While the cake is cooling, whip the cream for the middle of the cake to soft peaks. When the cake is cool, spread the jam evenly on one of the cakes and then dollop the whipped cream over the jam and spread out to the edges. Place the other layer of cake gently on top so the filling does not ooze out.

Sift the powdered sugar over the top of the cake covering it completely and serve.

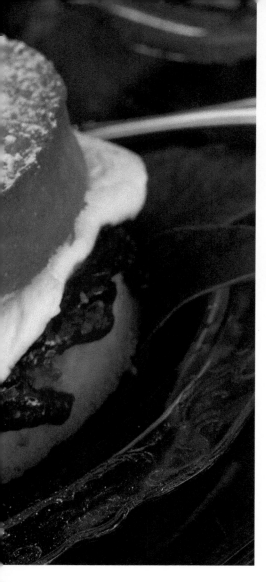

How to make the perfect pot of tea

Empty your kettle and fill it with freshly drawn water. Put the kettle on the heat and just before it comes to a boil, pour a generous dash of the hot water into your teapot, swirling it round and round inside the teapot before pouring it out. It may seem like a meaningless ritual, but it is not. This ensures that the water stays at the boiling point when it hits the tea, encouraging the proper opening of the leaves. Dole out one heaping teaspoon of tea leaves for each person and one for the pot straight into the warmed teapot. The water will have reached a galloping boil by this time, but take care that the water does not boil for long as it begins to lose oxygen and this will result in a bitter muddy brew of tea. Once you have poured the boiling water over the tea leaves in the pot, allow the tea to stand and brew for anywhere from three to six minutes according to the leaf size – less time for small leaves and more time for large leaves. Give the tea a good stir and pour it, using a strainer to catch the leaves. If you take your tea with milk, you should add it to the cup, cold and fresh before pouring the tea.

All about Sherry

Traditional sherry begins its life on vines originating from Spain and is made of three types of grapes native to the region. Only the first pressing of the grapes is used to produce sherry, a fortified wine. After the first fermentation, it is divided into three categories: The lightest and palest of the wines will be set aside to be turned into Fino and Amontillado, the slightly darker but still clean wine will be set aside to become Oloroso, a darker sherry. Sherry can be served as an aperitif or on its own, and also makes a great addition to cooking.

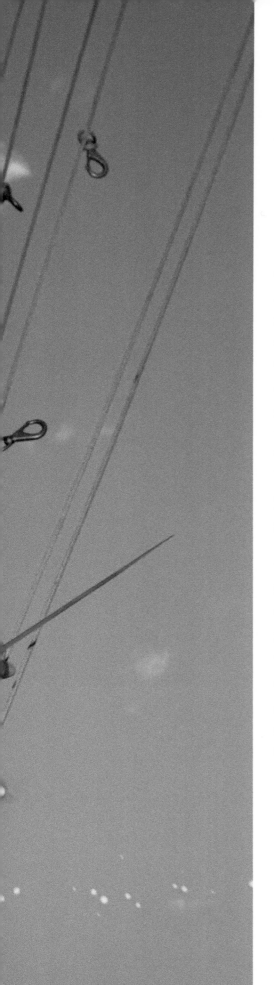

THE NEW 30
A 40th birthday party

A friend who was turning 40 chose to celebrate not by looking forward but by looking back and remembering his 30s because frankly, he was having a hard time turning that corner!

Our goal was to create a spectacular and wonderful party that would make this milestone a fond memory – chase away those "over-the-hill" thoughts. Psychologically, celebrating 40 as "the new 30" made him feel younger immediately. There was nothing old about what he saw for his party as he relayed his vision to us.

The event venue was set at a California marina, a spot for which he had fond childhood memories. He desired a dramatic look yet wanted the party itself, and the food, to be warm, inviting and comfortable. He had a few requests – that he create the playlist for the DJ, that there be a choice of his favorite drink, single-malt scotch, and that his birthday cake be our famous Three Milk Cake. All we had to do was add the details!

For the look, we began with a black and white palette and added a splash of spring green to symbolize youth. Sails became a sort of the theme for the party, so we placed 10-foot tall feather sails in black and white around the space. Solid white tables were used for the buffet, hung with green, black and white ribbons around the bases. The gentle bay breezes created a billowing effect which enhanced the theme of the party.

The menu of mac and cheese, stuffing cupcakes, corn salad, roasted pork and grilled lobster sandwiches tantalized the taste buds. We gave the birthday boy everything he wanted, and a little extra.

We added one more celebratory aspect – in a fun, funny and touching moment, after all the toasts and speeches were done, we dramatically opened a bottle of champagne for every decade … but we did so by "sabering" the bottle open with a huge knife. After all, what is turning 30, or even 40, without a little drama?

Menu

Preview
Asparagus Wrap
fresh asparagus wrapped in puff pastry ribbon

Grilled Shrimp Cocktail
grilled shrimp served with a
chimichurri cocktail sauce

Calamari Skewers
simple fresh calamari woven on a skewer
with a squeeze of fresh lime

Indulge
Three Milk Birthday Cake
sponge cake soaked with three milks
topped with poached gooseberries and a
dollop of whipped cream

Libation
Scotch Lounge
miniature bottles of single malt scotch
served with pitchers of water
and a bucket of ice

Main
Mac and Broccolini
macaroni and cheese with broccolini
individual servings kept hot on river rocks

Lobster Grilled Sandwich
grilled sourdough bread filled with lobster
and served with red bell pepper tartar

Yellow and White Corn Salad
grilled in the husk yellow and white corn
tossed with pearl couscous, fresh basil and tomatoes
in a lemon olive oil dressing

Roasted Pork Leg
carved roasted leg of pork with diamond scored
crackling served with sage pork gravy, petite stuffing
cupcakes topped with a mashed potato frosting and
garnished with a green olive

ASPARAGUS WRAP

Makes 24 pieces

24 asparagus spears

1 sheet puff pastry

4 tablespoons Boursin cheese

Egg Wash *(see recipe index)*

Cut asparagus spears into 3-inch long pieces and blanch in boiling water, pat dry and set aside. Use a rolling pin, roll out the puff pastry until it is paper thin and has almost doubled in size. Cut the pastry into 2x2½-inch rectangles. Discard the unused edges. Brush the pastry rectangles with egg wash covering the entire surface. Next, fill a piping bag with the softened Boursin cheese and pipe a thin line on one side of each puff pastry rectangle using approximately a ½ teaspoon of cheese on each one. Lay an asparagus spear on the Boursin cheese and roll it up in the puff pastry. Brush the outside of the rolled puff pastry with Egg Wash. Bake in an oven at 375 degrees for 10 to 15 minutes or until golden brown.

CALAMARI SKEWERS

Makes 24 skewers

12 calamari, cleaned and cut in half lengthwise

24 6-inch long bamboo skewers

½ cup Vegetable Marinade
(see recipe index)

½ cup lime juice

Salt and pepper to taste

Soak the handle side of the wooden skewers in water for 1 hour. This will keep them from burning on the grill. Weave the calamari onto the skewer making sure that the point of the skewer is covered. Marinate the skewers in the Vegetable Marinade for 1 hour. To prepare, remove skewers from the marinade and drizzle with a little lime juice and sprinkle with salt and pepper. Sear the skewers on a very hot griddle or on the grill for one minute on each side. When finished, drizzle with a little more lime juice and serve.

GRILLED SHRIMP COCKTAIL

Makes 24 shrimp cocktail

24 large shrimp (size 21/25), peeled and deveined with the tail left on

Chimichurri Sauce *(see recipe index)*

¾ cup Vegetable Marinade
(see recipe index)

1 box daikon sprouts

24 little white plastic plates for serving *(available on-line, we use www.sweetflavorfl.com)*

Lightly butterfly the large end of the shrimp so they will stand up on the plate. Marinate the shrimp in the Vegetable Marinade for 1 hour. The next day grill the shrimp for 3 minutes on each side. To assemble, place 1 tablespoon of Chimichurri Sauce in the bottom of each white box. Place one grilled shrimp on top of the Chimichurri, garnish with daikon sprouts and serve.

MACARONI AND CHEESE WITH BROCCOLINI

Makes 2 quart casserole or 24 individual hors d'oeuvres, ¼ cup per serving

¼ cup butter

¼ cup flour

2¼ cups milk

1 bay leaf

Salt and white pepper

2 cups cheddar cheese, shredded

½ cup parmesan cheese, shredded

1 cup Fontina or Swiss cheese, shredded

½ pound macaroni pasta, cooked until soft

½ cup heavy cream

1½ cups blanched, chopped broccolini, plus extra pieces for garnish on top

1½ cups toasted bread crumbs tossed in melted butter to cover the top

In a sauce pan, melt the butter then whisk in the flour to make a roux and cook over medium heat for a few minutes. Add the milk and bay leaf and whisk constantly on high flame until the mixture comes to a boil and starts to thicken. Turn down the heat and cook over low heat, whisking frequently for about 10 minutes. Season to taste with salt and white pepper. Fold in the cheeses while the sauce is still hot. Stir in the cream and bring to a creamy consistency.

Add the pre-cooked macaroni, while still hot, to the sauce. Fold in the blanched broccolini and put the mixture into a casserole dish or individual serving dishes. Sprinkle the toasted breadcrumbs over the top. Put into a 375 degree oven for about 10 to15 minutes until the breadcrumbs are browned. Remove from the oven and place another piece of broccolini on top to garnish, then serve.

LOBSTER GRILLED SANDWICH

Makes 10 whole sandwiches

5 lobster tails (8 to 10 ounces each, ½ lobster tail per sandwich)

4 quarts water

2 cups white wine

1 onion, chopped

1 carrot, chopped

1 stalk celery, chopped

2 teaspoons black peppercorns

3 cloves garlic, peeled

1 lemon, halved

1 bay leaf

1½ cups Red Bell Pepper Tartar *(recipe to follow)*

10 slices of mozzarella cheese

1 loaf sliced sourdough bread (20 slices)

½ pound butter, softened

Place the water, white wine, onion, carrot, celery, black peppercorns, bay leaf, garlic and the lemon (with the juice squeezed into the liquid) into a large stock pot and bring to a boil. Boil the liquid for 10 minutes to let the flavors infuse. Place the lobster tails in the liquid and poach for 10 minutes until they are a bright red color. Remove the tails, drain and place in the refrigerator to chill. When chilled, take the lobster meat out of the shells and slice it into nice, thin pieces. To assemble the sandwiches, lay the bread slices on a flat surface. Spread each slice with pink peppercorn tartar and then lay a slice of mozzarella cheese on each side of the sandwich. Lay lobster slices on the cheese, covering one side of the sandwich. Place the other slice of bread over to close the sandwich. Rub the outside of the bread with butter and grill the sandwiches on a panini maker, griddle or grill. To serve, cut off the crusts and cut into triangles.

Red Bell Pepper Tartar
Makes 2 cups

¼ cup roasted red bell pepper, diced

¼ cup green pickle relish

¼ cup minced shallots (2 ounces)

¼ cup sour cream

¼ cup parsley, chopped

2 tablespoons capers

½ teaspoon garlic

⅔ cup mayonnaise

Salt and white pepper, to taste

Mix all the ingredients together in a food processor and pulse lightly, leaving the sauce a little chunky. Sauce can be made a few days ahead and refrigerated.

YELLOW AND WHITE CORN SALAD

Makes 9 cups

2-3 ears yellow corn

2-3 ears white corn

½ cup Vegetable Marinade *(see recipe index)*

6 cups large cous cous *(recipe to follow)*

3 tablespoons fresh basil, chiffonade

10 ounces or 1 cup small heirloom tomatoes - keep whole or cut in half

½ cup Lemon Olive Oil Dressing *(recipe to follow)*

Cook the corn by one of two methods: Prepare on a grill by removing the silk from the corn ears, leaving the husk on. Rub each ear with Vegetable Marinade and then re-cover fully with the husk and place on a hot grill turning occasionally until the corn is done. Cut the corn kernels off the cob and chill. To prepare the corn on the stove top, cut the corn kernels off the cob and toss them in the vegetable marinade. Heat a sauté pan over medium-high heat and cook the corn until browned, remove from the heat and chill.

Meanwhile, make the Lemon Olive Oil Dressing and place in the refrigerator to chill. Next, prepare the cous cous and place in the refrigerator to chill. After the corn and cous cous are chilled, toss them together in a large bowl with the basil and tomatoes and mix in the dressing. Add salt and pepper to taste and serve.

Lemon Olive Oil Dressing

Makes ½ cup

½ teaspoon garlic

2 tablespoons Dijon mustard

1 tablespoon lemon juice

½ teaspoon pure lemon extract oil (available at specialty stores) or lemon juice

½ cup olive oil

Salt and pepper

Place garlic, mustard, lemon juice, and pure lemon extract oil (or lemon juice) in a food processor and blend well. Slowly add the olive oil while the machine is going and pulse until the dressing emulsifies. Add salt and pepper to taste. Adjust the other seasonings if needed.

Cous Cous

Makes 6 cups

2 cups large cous cous

2 tablespoons butter

3 cups chicken broth

Place a pot on high heat on the stove and sauté the cous cous in the butter until golden brown. Add the chicken broth, then cover the pan and continue to cook until it boils. Take the pan off the heat and cover with foil and place in a warm area for approximately 15 minutes until water is absorbed. Pour the cous cous onto a baking pan and spread it out, then place in the refrigerator to chill.

ROASTED PORK LEG

Serves 50 to 75 people

1 20-pound pork leg

2 carrots, cut into large cubes

2 stalks of celery, cut into large cubes

1 onion, cut into large cubes

6-10 garlic cloves

Take the leg of pork and score the back fat into 1-inch diamond shapes with a knife. Place one garlic clove into each of the corners of the diamond shapes around the leg of pork. Spread the vegetables on a baking pan and place the pork leg on top of them. Rub the pork with a little vegetable oil and sprinkle with salt and pepper. Cover the pork with foil and roast in a 200 degree oven for 15 hours. Remove the foil, turn the temperature up to 350 degrees and continue to roast for about 2 hours longer, until the skin gets crispy on the outside. Remove from the oven and let rest for about 30 minutes before serving.

SAGE PORK GRAVY

Makes 2 quarts

2½ pounds pork meat, cut into large cubes

5 pounds pork shoulder bones

2 carrots, cut into 1-inch pieces

2 onions, cut into 1-inch pieces

½ bunch celery, cut into 1-inch pieces

Olive oil

Salt and pepper

1 gallon water

3 bay leaves

½ bunch thyme

½ bunch parsley stems

1 bunch sage

Roux (made of 1¼ cups flour and ¼ pound softened butter)

Place the pork cube meat, shoulder bones and vegetables on 3 seperate sheet pans and drizzle with a little olive oil, salt and pepper. Roast in a 350 degree oven for about 20 to 30 minutes. Remove vegetables and pork cubes and continue roasting shoulder bones another 10 to 15 minutes until golden brown.

Remove from the oven and place into a large heavy sauce pot. Deglaze the sheet pans with water, then add this liquid to the pot as well. Add the water, bay leaves, thyme, parsley stems and sage to the pot and bring to a boil, lower heat and simmer for 4 hours.

Skim the fat off the top and strain the broth through a sieve. Put the strained broth back into the pot and cook a little longer until it starts to thicken.

To make the broth thicker, add the roux. Be sure to add the roux slowly and whisk until you get a gravy like consistency. Season with salt and pepper and serve.

STUFFING CUPCAKE WITH MASH POTATO FROSTING WITH A GREEN OLIVE GARNISH

Makes 32 medium cupcakes, ⅓ cup stuffing per serving

Stuffing

2 pounds plain focaccia, cut in ¾-inch cubes

½ pound butter

4 cups yellow onions, diced

2 cups celery, diced

4 teaspoons poultry seasoning

2 cups chicken broth

½ cup parsley, finely chopped

¼ cup sage, finely chopped

¼ cup thyme, finely chopped

Salt and pepper to taste

Mashed potatoes

9 large russet potatoes

⅔ cup heavy cream

1 tablespoon roasted garlic puree

½ pound butter, softened

Salt and white pepper to taste

Garnish

32 small whole green olives

Lay the focaccia cubes on a tray and dry them in the oven for 10 to 15 minutes at 300 degrees. Meanwhile, melt the butter in a sauce pan, add onions and celery and cook over low heat until very tender. Add the poultry seasoning and set aside. Mix together bread, chicken broth, parsley, sage, thyme, salt, pepper and the celery and onion mixture in a large bowl. Grease medium muffin pans and fill each with ⅓ cup of filling. Cover with foil and bake in the oven at 350 degrees for 30 to 35 minutes. Take the foil off and bake for an additional 15 minutes until crispy and golden brown.

While the cupcakes are baking, prepare the potatoes. Peel the potatoes and cut each one into large pieces. Put the potatoes in a pot of water with salt and bring to a boil. Cook for about 30 minutes or until soft. Strain water from the pot and put potatoes back into the pot. Mash the potatoes and then add the cream, garlic, butter, margarine, salt and white pepper.

To assemble, take a stuffing cupcake and 'frost' it with the mashed potatoes. You can spread the potatoes on with a knife or put the mashed potatoes in a piping bag and pipe them on top. Garnish with a green olive and serve.

THREE MILK CAKE WITH POACHED GOOSEBERRIES AND WHIPPED CREAM

Makes one 10-inch cake

Cake

2 cups all-purpose flour

4 teaspoons baking powder

6 eggs, separated

¼ teaspoon cream of tartar

2 cups sugar

½ cup milk

1 cup heavy cream

1 can evaporated milk (12-ounce)

1 can sweetened condensed milk (14-ounce)

Whipped Cream

2 cups heavy cream

¼ cup powdered sugar

Poached Gooseberries

1 pound green gooseberries, cleaned

2 quarts Simple Syrup *(see recipe index)*

Sift together flour and baking powder and set aside. With a kitchen mixer, beat the egg whites and cream of tartar until foamy. With the mixer on high speed, gradually add the sugar. Next, beat in the yolks, one at a time. Add ¼ of the flour mixture and mix well, repeat with each ¼ of the mixture, mixing well each time. Scrape the bowl and add the milk and mix until well blended. Pour into a baking pan that has been sprayed with non-stick spray and lined with parchment paper. Bake in a 350 degree oven for 30 minutes, then turn down the oven to 325 degrees and bake 45 minutes longer or until a toothpick inserted into the cake comes out clean. Remove the cake and let cool for 10 minutes in the pan.

While the cake is baking, mix the heavy cream, evaporated milk and condensed milk in a bowl. With a skewer, poke holes all over the cake at 1-inch intervals. Pour the milk mixture all over the cake slowly until all the liquid is absorbed. Place the cake in the refrigerator and cool for at least 1 hour or overnight.

Poach gooseberries by gently simmering them in the simple syrup in a pan for 10 minutes. Strain the gooseberries from the simple syrup and set aside to chill.

To serve, remove the cake from the refrigerator and unmold it onto a platter with a deep rim so that the milk doesn't leak over the edge. Make the whipped cream and frost the cake liberally with it, top with Poached Gooseberies.

How to Saber a Champagne Bottle

It has been said that Napoleon was the first to take his saber to a bottle of champagne in order to open it and that he did so after each victory in battle. This tells us that not only do the French know champagne, they also know a thing or two about style. So, if you are interested in assuming some French style, here is a little advice about sabering a bottle.

First, a saber is a sword but, for these purposes we use a large regular kitchen knife. We use the back of the knife instead of the sharp side. Start with a well chilled bottle of champagne as the 'saber' will actually be used to break the head off the bottle and cold glass makes for a cleaner break with less mess and fewer shards of glass. Unwrap the bottle by removing the wire twisted over the cork and all the aluminum foil. You should take the 'saber' up the entire side of the bottle along the seam, in one clean sweep. In order to stem the loss of any champagne, hold the bottle at a 45-degree angle with your left hand (use your right hand if you are left handed).

Begin moving the 'saber' swiftly and evenly from the bottom of the bottle up to the top and through the rim in one clean motion. Don't twist. Don't be afraid. Be confident and in control. There will be no glass in the bottle once you have completed the move because the pressure of the break blows everything away from the bottle. But DO be careful of where you aim the bottle! Once you have neatly sabered the bottle open, pour yourself a glass, but watch those sharp edges!

Personalizing the Party

We believe that every party needs to include a detail that gives guests a little insight into the host or hostess. At this event, we dressed the staff in T-shirts that conveyed information about the host. We also created a "library" setting in which to display a selection of single-malt scotches (the birthday boy's favorite drink). Putting your own personalized stamp on your event can be as small as choosing colors that have personal meaning to you, bringing in an entertainment element or even creating a menu that reflects your childhood or your present-day concerns, such as the environment. Whatever it is, dig deep to find that certain detail that will make your party special and memorable and most of all, all about you.

CALIFORNIA BAJA
Poolside

After Christian and Janie installed a backyard pool to beat the heat of California, they realized that their landscaping had not escaped the toll that months of messy construction can take. After administering heavy doses of 'TLC' to the yard and keeping watch as it bloomed and came back to life, it was time for that very Californian phenomenon – the pool party. The fact that there was a pool and this was a party were the only rules we had in creating this evening. For instance, most pool parties favor colored acrylic glasses and plates. Not here. We used glassware, a glass table, a glass chandelier and even chairs that looked like glass (but were actually acrylic). We are happy to report that nothing but a few pre-conceived notions were broken during the night!

Eschewing the traditional colors of summer, we chose to accent the party with purple and teal. To me, these colors feel icy cool and that was the ambience we were going for. Plus, they fit into the surroundings perfectly. Sometimes you have to go against common sense and let the environment dictate your look. We placed a runner made of flowers across the center of the table and made a small floral arrangement for each place setting. A linen napkin placed over the back of each chair added a splash of color as the table was clear glass. The pool was lit and washed with a deep blue color and purple uplights were placed throughout the garden. We bathed the table in purple lighting which made the glass glisten and gave the chandelier a watery effect.

The signature drink was officially called a mojito but we gave that a twist too by using purple basil, rum and honeydew with a sugar cane stir stick. The menu featured such traditional items as seafood tacos and ceviche made with local, sustainable fish but we broke the rules again by serving soft shell crab (usually used for appetizers) as the main course. For dessert, a coconut crème caramel with a watermelon soup lent a clean – and colorful – freshness to the end of the meal.

This party illustrates my main philosophy on décor and menu design – "rules" are made to be broken. We actually served the wine in a martini style glass because it looked "cool," another rule broken. The only rule that I feel is important to follow at a pool party is to wait half an hour before jumping into the water!

Menu

Preview
Tortilla Seafood Taco
tortilla topped with shrimp and squid with cilantro,
grilled pineapple and fresh lime juice

Begin
Trio of Ceviche
grilled shrimp, crab, jicama, green apple, radish

salmon, cucumber, pickled pink
peppercorns, Thai basil

scallop, yam, coconut, raisin, cilantro
served in baked five spiced tortilla cones

Main
Crispy Soft Shell Crab
crispy soft shell crab served with lobster salad with
lettuce, avocado, and heirloom tomato tossed in a
chipotle fresh lime dressing with savory soft polenta

Indulge
Coconut Crème Caramel Flan
creamy crème caramel with toasted coconut served
with a candied lemon swizzle stick and
chilled watermelon soup

Libation
Honeydew Purple Basil Mojito

FOOD FUN LOVE

TORTILLA SEAFOOD TACO

Makes 1½ cups taco filling to make 24 small tacos

½ pound fresh shrimp, cleaned and deveined, cut into a small dice

1 cup fresh lime juice

½ cup fresh squid, cleaned and chopped into a small dice (keep legs separate)

½ cup fresh red tomatoes, diced

¼ cup radishes, diced

⅓ cup cucumber, diced

½ bunch of cilantro, chopped

½ pineapple, sliced

Salt and pepper

3 10-inch flour tortillas, cut with a 2½-inch cutter into circles to make a small basket. You will get about 8 circles per tortilla. (You can also shape the tortilla into a taco form or tostada if you like.)

Marinate the shrimp in 1 cup of lime juice overnight to "cook." The next day add the squid to the shrimp and marinate for an additional 2 hours. In a separate container marinate the squid legs in 1 cup of lime juice for two hours. Meanwhile, prepare the pineapple by grilling the slices on a grill. Cut into a small dice and chill.

After the two hours, strain the lime juice from both the shrimp and squid mixture and squid legs and set aside. The squid legs should remain separate to be used as garnish for the taco.

Add the diced tomatoes, radishes, cucumber, cilantro and chilled pineapple to the shrimp and squid mixture. Add some salt and pepper to taste and a little more lime juice to taste. Set aside.

Next, prepare the tortillas. To make the tortilla basket, take the cut tortilla circle and place it in between two small ladles. Dip the ladles with the tortilla into a fryer for 3 minutes until golden brown. Pull the ladles apart, remove the tortilla, and place back in the fryer for another minute if the middle is not fully cooked. Remove and lay the tortilla basket on paper towels to drain. When the baskets cool, spoon in the shrimp and squid mixture and garnish with the legs of the squid and a sprig of cilantro.

TRIO OF CEVICHE SERVED IN FIVE SPICED TORTILLA CONES

Ceviche of Shrimp and Crab with Jicama, Green Apple and Radish
Makes 1½ quarts

1 pound (2 cups) shrimp, peeled and deveined

½ pound (1½ cups) cooked crab, broken up into small pieces

1 cup jicama, diced

1 cup green apple, diced

¾ cup radish, diced

1 small bunch scallions

1 cup cucumber, diced

2 cups lime juice

Salt and pepper to taste

Chop the shrimp into small pieces and put in a bowl with the lime juice to marinate overnight. The next day, add the crab meat and place back in the refrigerator for 1 hour. Drain the lime juice and mix in the jicama, green apple, radish, scallions, cucumber and salt and pepper to taste. Let the ceviche sit for 1 hour. Check the seasons again and serve.

Seared Salmon Ceviche with Cucumber, Pickled Pink Peppercorns and Thai Basil
Makes 1 quart

1 tablespoon pink peppercorns marinated in rice wine vinegar

2 pounds fresh salmon filet, no skin or bones

Olive oil

1 cup lime juice

3 cups cucumber, diced

1 cup roasted yellow pepper, chopped

2 teaspoons Aji pepper paste *(available in Latin markets)*

½ ounce Thai basil, chiffonade

Salt and pepper to taste

Marinate the pink peppercorns a day before. First bang on the peppercorns a little to open them and then marinate them in about 2 tablespoons rice wine vinegar overnight in a container at room temperature.

Season the salmon with salt and pepper and sear on high heat in a sauté pan with a little olive oil for about 2 minutes on each side. Set aside to cool. Once the salmon has cooled, chop into small pieces and marinate in lime juice over night.

The next day, strain the salmon and add the pickled pink peppercorns (drained from the rice wine vinegar), cucumber, roasted yellow pepper, Aji pepper paste and Thai basil. Check seasonings and adjust to taste if needed. Marinate in the refrigerator for about 1 hour and serve.

Scallop Ceviche with Yam, Coconut, Raisins and Cilantro
Makes 1½ quarts

2 yams, peeled and finely diced

Olive oil

1 pound bay scallops, cut in half

1 cup fresh lime juice

⅓ cup sweetened shredded coconut

¼ cup red onion, finely diced

¼ cup raisins

¼ cup coconut milk

2 tablespoons fresh cilantro, chopped

Salt and black pepper to taste

Blanch the yams in boiling water with a little salt until just soft. Remove from the water and spread out onto a sheet tray. Roast them in the oven with a little olive oil at 350 degrees for 10 to 15 minutes until they are golden brown. Remove from the oven and set aside.

In a bowl, mix the scallops with the lime juice, tossing lightly. Cover the bowl with plastic wrap and refrigerate for at least 30 minutes to 1 hour. Meanwhile, spread the shredded coconut on a baking sheet and toast in a 350 degree oven until golden brown, about 5 minutes, stirring every few minutes so that the coconut toasts evenly. Remove and set aside.

Drain the scallops and transfer to a clean bowl, then add the yams, onion, raisins, coconut milk, cilantro and salt and pepper to taste. Mix well and refrigerate for at least 30 minutes and up to 3 hours. Garnish with the toasted coconut and whole cilantro leaves and serve.

Five Spiced Tortilla Cones
Makes 16 cones

1½ teaspoons paprika

1 tablespoon Mexican achiote paste

¼ teaspoon cayenne pepper

1 teaspoon salt

3 tablespoons fresh lime juice

⅓ cup vegetable oil

4 12-inch flour tortillas

Flour and water glue mixture

Metal cornet molds

Pieces of aluminum foil

1 tablespoon paprika

1 teaspoon cayenne pepper

In a bowl, mix together paprika, achiote paste, cayenne pepper, salt, lime juice and oil, set aside. Cut the tortillas into 10-inch circles. Brush both sides of the tortilla with the oil mixture and then cut each circle into quarters (this provides for a clean edge to the cones). Prepare metal cornet molds by wrapping the large open end with a folded strip of aluminum foil to widen the opening of the cones. Roll a tortilla triangle around the cone shape. Take some flour and mix with a little water to make a paste and put a little on the edge of the tortilla triangle so that it sticks together in the cone shape.

Place cones seam side down on a sheet pan. Bake at 300 degrees for 8 minutes. Take the mold out of the tortilla cones and bake for approximately 10 minutes longer or until completely crispy. The tortilla cones should be light brown and crisp. Mix paprika and cayenne pepper together and sprinkle on top of the cones after they are cooked. Cones can be stored in an airtight container at room temperature for up to one week.

CRISPY SOFT SHELL CRAB

Makes 10 servings

1 pound mâche

½ cup Chipotle Lime Dressing *(recipe to follow)*

4 quarts water

2 cups white wine

1 carrot, chopped

1 white onion, chopped

1 stalk celery, chopped

1 whole lemon, cut in half

3 cloves of garlic

Small handful of black peppercorns

5 lobster tails (8 to 10 ounces each)

10 fresh soft shell crabs (4 to 5 ounces each) with its glands and stomach cut out

Tempura batter *(recipe to follow)*

8 cups Savory Soft Polenta *(recipe to follow)*

5 ripe avocados, cut in half and sliced

3 10-ounce baskets of baby heirloom tomato medley, cut in half

Make a poaching liquid with water, white wine, carrot, onion, celery, lemon, garlic and black peppercorns and boil for 10 minutes to infuse the flavors. Add the lobster and boil for 8 to 10 minutes until lobster turns red. Remove the lobster from the liquid and set aside. Let the tails cool slightly and then remove the meat from the shells and slice into thick slices. Set aside.

Prepare the soft shell crab by dipping the crabs into the tempura batter, coating each side well. Fry them in hot oil approximately 5 minutes until golden brown. Place the crabs on paper towels to drain off excess oil.

Toss the mâche lightly with chipotle dressing, salt and pepper and set aside.

To assemble, place the slices from half a lobster tail on the side of the plate, shingling the slices so that they are in a fan pattern. Top with a large spoonful of the mâche. Next, spoon ¾ cup of polenta on the other side of the plate and top with a hot soft shell crab. Place the sliced avocado in a fan design next to the polenta and lay the tomato halves next to the avocado.

Savory Soft Polenta

Makes 8 cups

2½ cups polenta (yellow cornmeal)

10 cups chicken broth

Black pepper

2 tablespoons butter

2 roasted serrano chilies, peeled, deseeded and finely chopped

1 cup sautéed shallots

1 cup grilled corn

2 cups parmesan cheese, grated

Combine the polenta and broth in a saucepan. Cook over high heat, stirring constantly, until the mixture comes to a boil. Continue to cook over high heat, stirring constantly with a wooden spoon, for 15 to 20 minutes, until creamy. Take the pan off the heat and season with pepper and finish with a little butter. Add in the serrano chilies, shallots, corn and cheese, stirring until the cheese is melted. Serve immediately.

Chipotle Lime Dressing

Makes approximately 1 cup

2 tablespoons white wine vinegar

1 teaspoon minced garlic

½ teaspoon achiote paste

1 teaspoon minced chipotle chili

1 teaspoon Dijon mustard

¼ teaspoon ground black pepper

¾ cup mayonnaise

2 tablespoons lime juice

¼ cup olive oil

In a food processor, pulse all the ingredients except the olive oil until blended. Add the olive oil slowly and continue to puree until the dressing is smooth. Check the seasoning and adjust if needed.

Tempura Batter

Makes 1½ cups for 10 softshell crabs

¾ cup rice flour

¼ cup cornstarch

½ teaspoon baking powder

¼ teaspoon baking soda

2 egg whites

1 teaspoon salt

1 cup water

Combine all ingredients in a large bowl and mix until well blended.

COCONUT CRÈME CARAMEL FLAN

Makes 12 flans, 4 ounces each

Caramel

1¼ cups sugar

⅛ cup water

Custard

4 eggs

2 egg yolks

¼ cup granulated sugar

1 teaspoon vanilla extract

1 cup coconut milk

2 cups half and half

½ cup heavy cream

Shaved toasted coconut to garnish

Prepare the flan containers by placing them in a large pan deep enough to hold a couple inches of hot water later to create a water bath. To prepare the caramel, melt the sugar and water over low heat in a medium saucepan and stir until the syrup is clear. Then turn heat up and cook the syrup until it is golden brown but not dark in color. Brush down the sugar crystals on the sides of the pan with a wet pastry brush as they form. When the caramel is ready, pour approximately two tablespoons into each mold. Work very fast and be careful, the caramel will be very hot and sticky. Let the caramel set while you make the custard.

In a mixing bowl, whisk together the eggs, egg yolks, sugar, vanilla, milk, half and half and cream. Pour the custard into the molds over the caramel, filling almost to the top. Pour hot water into the pan around the flan cups to create the water bath. Bake in a regular oven at 300 degrees for about 50 minutes or until a knife comes out clean when inserted into the custard. Chill overnight to firm.

Turn custard over onto a serving plate. Garnish with shaved toasted coconut.

WATERMELON SOUP

Makes 4 cups

⅔ cup granulated sugar

⅔ cup water

1 piece lemon rind, 1x2 inches

½ cinnamon stick

½ of a vanilla bean

2 pounds fresh watermelon

¾ cup sweet late harvest Riesling or Muscat dessert wine

Bring the sugar and water to a boil in a sauce pan, stirring until the sugar is dissolved. Add the lemon rind, cinnamon and vanilla and boil again for a couple of minutes. Take off the heat, cool and then strain. In a food processor, puree the watermelon and sugar water mixture together. Mix with the wine and then chill. Serve cold in a shot glass with swizzle stick. Note: Soup can be made a day ahead.

LEMON SWIZZLE STICKS
Makes 12 12-inch swizzle sticks

Lemon Simple Syrup

½ cup sugar

½ cup water

Zest from 5 lemons, grated

2 teaspoons lemon extract

Candy Zest

2 cups sugar

⅓ cup of water

Long zest strips from 6 lemons

Sticks

1 sheet puff pastry

¼ cup crystal sugar

To make the Lemon Simple Syrup, combine the sugar, water, lemon zest and lemon extract in a pot. Boil for 5 minutes until the syrup is slightly reduced. Remove the pot from the heat and chill.

To make the Candy Zest, combine 1 cup of sugar and water in a pot and bring to a boil over medium heat. Once it is boiling, add the zest and lower the heat. Cook the mixture until it is translucent and then strain out the lemon zest. In a separate bowl, take the remaining 1 cup of sugar and toss in the cooked lemon zest to coat with sugar. Sift out the zest. Place the zest back into the bowl of sugar again to coat for a second time. Sift out the zest again and lay them on a sheet pan to let them dry and absorb the sugar. When dry, chop the zest into small pieces.

To make the sticks, brush the puff pastry sheet on both sides with the lemon simple syrup. Sprinkle the pastry sheet with crystal sugar and the candy zest on both sides. Cut the pastry sheet into 12 long strips. Twist each strip and place on a sheet pan lined with parchment paper and put in the freezer until they harden. Bake in the oven at 300 degrees for 10 to 15 minutes until the sticks are golden and crisp.

PURPLE BASIL
HONEYDEW MOJITO

Makes 1 serving

2 ounces honeydew melon juice

3 purple basil leaves

½ ounce Simple Syrup *(see recipe index)*

2 ounces silver rum

1 ounce club soda

Ice

Fresh sugar cane sticks
(available from specialty markets)

Juice some fresh honeydew melon with a
juicer and set aside. Muddle the purple
basil leaves with Simple Syrup in a glass.
Add the honeydew melon juice, rum,
club soda and ice to the glass, stir
together. Garnish with sugar cane and a
thin slice of melon and serve.

The Power of Lighting

I cannot over-emphasize the power that lighting brings to a party or gathering. It provides the impact that becomes the final "wow" factor. Because it is so important, I advise people to allow a budget for lighting to highlight the main areas of the party, such as the dance floor, bars, buffets, architectural elements and guest tables. Pin-spotting each table with its own overhead light is extremely effective. If your budget does not allow for that, try working with a rental company to provide a color wash in the main areas in amber or lavender light, both colors make everyone look great. The addition of votive candles can also create warmth and ambient lighting.

An easy at-home trick is to simply change the bulbs in your lamps to colored ones. Also, if you aren't working with a rental company or professional lighting company, you can purchase clip-on lights and fit them with a colored bulbs that match the color scheme of your party. Clip them high up in a tree or other tall object so that they cannot be easily seen and they will definitely add that sexy look to your party.

Luminaries also make a statement as they can be used to create a lighted path if you need to direct your guests. For safety reasons, always place candles in glass cylinders with the flame at least two inches from the top. Battery operated votive candles are an option that are readily available and cost effective these days. They are a great substitute for candles and usually have 70 hours of life. One more way to add lighting is to add a personal touch with a projection on your dance floor or driveway of your name, the party name, a design or a logo. In the event industry, these are called gobos – metal die cuts that can easily be custom produced by lighting companies and are often available online at places like www.goboman.com.

Whether you choose to get creative with lighting or not, you should at least consider it – parties and guests all look better in the right light.

A SUNDAY KIND OF LOVE
A *time to be you*

You would think that after a week of creating parties for people I'd want a day off. But that is not the case. I actually look forward to Sundays when I can spend time with friends and family and create my own parties. It's the one day when I can renew my passion for food and wine and explore all the new recipes and ideas that have been swimming around in my head all week. It seems that over the years I have surrounded myself with like-minded people, so a gathering at either my home or a friends' home is where you will find me sharing the moments that make it a 'Sunday Kind of Love'.

Our friends, Janette and Bruce, have a beautiful home in the mountains overlooking the ocean. They grow lemons, herbs and vegetables and have a love for the alfresco lifestyle that California's weather affords us. This particular Sunday, Janette and I decided to prepare a meal together while our husbands played golf. We had planned the menu and shopped for ingredients in advance because once you are on that mountain, provisions are a long way off. But, most of the ingredients for the meal came straight from her abundant garden. We even made our own liqueur! Janette, a great home chef, is also an expert at making limoncello, an Italian after-dinner drink, and taught me how to do it as well.

We cooked up a storm as we listened to light opera, caught up with talk of our kids, set the table, picked flowers and pottered around the kitchen, preparing a beautiful meal for our husbands and our invited guests. In the late afternoon, with everyone gathered around, we began Sunday dinner with a sparkling limoncello martini. And as the sun set, dinner was served and A Sunday Kind of Love was felt all around.

Menu

Antipasti
Herbed Breadsticks
served with
Tomato, basil and garlic,
roasted eggplant caponata

White capellini beans, green olive tapenade

Artichoke, tomato and sweet pea stew

Begin
Heirloom Tomato Caprese
fresh italian burrata and tomato two ways,
oven baked as well as sliced fresh, layered with crispy
basil and a drizzle of sweet balsamic reduction

Libation
Sparkling Limoncello Martini
sparkling Italian wine with Limoncello
and a lavender sprig

Main
Osso Buco
served family style
traditionally braised lamb shanks with red wine,
herbs, tomatoes, shallots, carrots and celery

Fennel Asparagus Risotto
creamy arborio rice blended with parmesan,
butter, white wine, chopped asparagus, shallots,
fennel and thyme

Grilled Vegetables
grilled cremini mushrooms, white rose
potatoes, yellow and orange peppers,
yellow summer squash,
zucchini and green onions

Indulge
Panna Cotta Blueberry
timbale of white chocolate panna cotta with blueberries
and their syrup served with hazelnut biscotti
and Christine cookies

HERBED BREADSTICKS

Makes 25 5-inch breadsticks

2 cups all-purpose flour

½ tablespoon salt

½ tablespoon yeast

2 tablespoons roasted garlic puree

1 red bell pepper, roasted, peeled and pureed

¼ cup olive oil

¼ cup cold water

1¼ cups mixed herbs (chopped rosemary, thyme, parsley and chive)

Blend flour, salt, yeast, garlic, bell pepper purée and ¼ cup herbs together with a kitchen mixer using the dough hook attachment. Slowly add the olive oil and water simultaneously, while still mixing, until a doughy consistency is achieved. Knead the dough for 15 minutes longer in the mixer. Put the dough in a greased bowl, cover with a damp cloth, put in a warm place and let it rise until the dough is doubled in size. This takes about 45 minutes to 1 hour.

Once the dough has risen, remove it from the bowl and start rolling out the dough by hand. Roll into breadsticks that are 5 inches long and a ½-inch wide. Lightly roll breadsticks in the remaining herbs.

Place the breadsticks on a sheet pan that is coverd with parchment paper and bake in a 300 degree oven for 15 to 20 minutes until crisp but not brown.

ROASTED EGGPLANT CAPONATA

Makes 2 cups

2 eggplants

1 tablespoon olive oil

1½ tablespoons garlic, minced

1 cup diced tomatoes (canned)

1 cup tomato juice

1½ teaspoons rosemary, chopped

1½ teaspoons thyme, chopped

1 teaspoon ground black pepper

Slice eggplant into ½-inch thick slices and lay on a baking pan. Sprinkle with salt and let rest covered in the refrigerator for 1 hour or overnight. Squeeze the water from the eggplant slices with paper towels. In a pan, sauté the garlic in olive oil and then add the eggplant and the remaining ingredients and simmer for approximately 1 hour. Check the seasoning and adjust if necessary then mash with a masher. Refrigerate until ready to serve.

WHITE CAPELLINI BEAN TOPPING

Makes 2 cups

1 cup white beans, dry

¼ cup carrot, diced into 1-inch cubes

¼ cup celery, diced into 1-inch cubes

½ cup onion, diced into 1-inch cubes

2 cups chicken broth

2 cups water

1 tablespoon olive oil

1 tablespoon chopped parsley

1 tablespoon roasted garlic

Rinse the white beans and set aside. Sauté carrots, celery, and onions in olive oil in a pot over high heat. Add the beans, chicken broth and water. Bring to a boil and reduce to a simmer and cook 1 hour until the beans are tender and soft. Add salt and pepper to taste and chill in the refrigerator until cooled. Remove the beans from the refrigerator, drain the liquid and place in a food processor. Add the olive oil, parsley and roasted garlic and puree. Topping can be left a little chunky if you prefer.

TOMATO, BASIL AND GARLIC TOPPING

Makes 2 cups

¾ pound heirloom tomatoes, diced (approximately 6 tomatoes)

1 tablespoon fresh basil, chiffonade

1 tablespoon balsamic vinegar

1 teaspoon garlic, minced

2 tablespoons extra virgin olive oil

Salt and pepper to taste

Mix all the ingredients together in a bowl and serve. This must be made the same day that it is served because it will lose its freshness overnight

GREEN OLIVE TAPENADE

Makes 2 cups

1 cup large Spanish queen green olives, drained

1 cup green pimento stuffed cocktail olives, drained

2 garlic cloves, peeled

1 bunch fresh rosemary

2½ cups extra virgin olive oil

1 tablespoon garlic, minced

¾ cup parsley, chopped

¼ teaspoon dried crushed red pepper

1 teaspoon ground black pepper

1 tablespoon mustard seeds

1 tablespoon lemon juice

The day before, mix the olives, whole garlic cloves, 2 whole rosemary stems and 2 cups of the olive oil together in a bowl and marinate overnight, making sure the marinade covers the olives completely. Strain the olives, reserving the liquid, and remove any pits with an olive pitter. Place the olives, minced garlic, parsley, 1 tablespoon chopped rosemary (stems removed) and ¼ cup of the olive oil in a food processor and pulse until lightly pureed but not smooth. Put the tapenade in a bowl and add in the mustard seed, lemon juice and 1 tablespoon of olive oil and stir, making sure to mix well.

ARTICHOKE, TOMATO AND SWEET PEA STEW

Makes 2 cups

2 tablespoons olive oil

1½ teaspoons garlic, minced

1½ teaspoons butter

1 can (15-ounce) artichoke bottoms, diced into ½-inch squares

¾ cup diced tomatoes, canned

½ cup Sun-Dried Tomato Sauce *(recipe to follow)*

½ cup frozen sweet peas

Heat olive oil, garlic and butter in a sauté pan. Stir in the artichokes and diced tomatoes in small amounts and heat through. Mix in the Sun-Dried Tomato Sauce and heat through. Add the sweet peas, heat through and serve.

Sun-Dried Tomato Sauce
Makes ½ cup

1 tablespoon red wine vinegar

1 teaspoon white sugar

1½ cups chicken broth

½ cup shallots, finely chopped

2 tablespoons celery, chopped

1 tablespoon carrot, chopped

1 tablespoon sun-dried tomatoes, chopped

2 tablespoons butter

2 tablespoons all-purpose flour

2 tablespoons white wine

Salt and pepper

Combine the red wine vinegar and sugar in a sauce pan and bring to a boil. Reduce the heat and simmer until the sauce is reduced by half. Add the chicken broth and bring to a boil again, take the pan off the heat and set aside. In another saucepan, over medium heat, sauté the shallots, celery, carrots and sun-dried tomatoes in butter for about 10 minutes until translucent and golden brown. Season with a little salt and pepper. Reduce the heat, add the flour and cook for 7 more minutes over low heat until the flour is cooked out.

Add the wine and continue to cook over low heat to reduce the sauce for 5 minutes longer. Add the broth mixture to the sun-dried tomato mixture and continue to cook over low heat for 1 hour. Strain the sauce and season to taste.

HEIRLOOM TOMATO CAPRESE
Makes 10 servings

4 large heirloom tomatoes, variety of colors

2 baskets baby heirloom medley tomatoes (8 to10-ounces each)

10 servings Baked Roma Tomatoes *(recipe to follow)*

¼ cup balsamic glaze *(available at specialty stores)*

5 fresh Ovoline mozzarella cheese, cut in half

1 pint Burrata cheese

1 bunch fresh basil

Salt and pepper

¼ cup Basil Oil *(recipe to follow)*

10 3-inch skewers

Cut the large heirloom tomatoes into wedges and different interesting shapes. Cut the medley tomatoes in half or keep them whole. Make the Baked Roma Tomatoes.

Take the balsamic glaze and drizzle it on one side of the plate. Take half of a mozzarella cheese, place it on the glaze, then place a leaf of fresh basil on top and one of the Baked Roma Tomatoes on top of that. Put a 3-inch skewer straight down through the center to hold them together.

On the other side of the plate, place a scoop of Burrata cheese and lay the heirloom tomatoes on and around it. Sprinkle the whole plate with salt and pepper. Drizzle with basil oil and garnish with Fried Basil Garnish *(recipe to follow)* and serve.

Baked Roma Tomato
Makes 10 servings, ½ tomato per serving

5 Roma tomatoes

¼ cup olive oil

salt and pepper

Zest of 1 lemon

¼ cup mixed herbs (parsley, thyme, rosemary, mint, dill and chives, chopped and mixed together)

¼ cup powdered sugar

Blanch tomatoes in simmering water and peel the skin off. Cut the tomatoes in half and toss in the olive oil. Lay them on a baking sheet with cut end up. Sprinkle generously with salt and pepper, grated lemon zest and the chopped herb mixture and then sift all of the powdered sugar over them. Place in the oven at 300 degrees and bake for 4 to 6 hours until the tomatoes are dry.

Basil Oil
Makes 1 quart

1 quart extra virgin olive oil

1 ounce or handful of fresh basil

Take the fresh basil and rub it together with your hands to break it up and bring out the flavor. Place the basil in a pot with the olive oil and warm the oil slightly over a very low heat. After about 5 minutes, take the oil off the stove and let it cool. When cooled, place into a container. Basil oil will stay fresh for weeks in an air-tight container.

Fried Basil Garnish

Heat oil to 300 degrees in a heavy pan. Fry leftover basil leaves until crispy, about 5 minutes. Remove from the oil and drain on a paper towel to cool.

OSSO BUCO

Makes 10 servings

10 veal shanks (about 1 pound), center cut, 2 inches thick

1 cup all-purpose flour for dusting the shanks + ½ cup flour for sauce

1½ cups olive oil

⅔ cup carrots, finely diced

3 stalks celery, finely diced

2 cups onion, finely diced

Fine sea salt

2 tablespoons garlic, minced

Freshly ground black pepper

4 cups dry red wine

2½ cups tomato sauce *(recipe to follow)*

12 cups veal or chicken stock

6 ounces dried porcini mushrooms, soaked in hot water and strained - reserve the liquid

Zest of 3 lemons

1 cup glace de viande
(recipe to follow, also available in specialty stores)

1 bouquet of garni consisting of 1 fresh rosemary sprig, 1 fresh sage leaf, 1 garlic clove, 1 bay leaf tied in a cheesecloth bundle

¼ cup chopped Italian parsley

Tie each of the veal shanks together separately so that each shank holds together. Toss the shanks in 1 cup of the flour so that they are evenly coated. Heat 2 tablespoons of the olive oil in a pot and add the shanks and brown well on all sides, adding more oil as needed. Remove the shanks from the pot and set aside. In the same pan, reduce the heat to medium-low and add the remaining olive oil, carrots, celery, onion, garlic and cook, stirring constantly, until the vegetables are softened, about 10 minutes. Add the remaining ½ cup of flour to thicken the mixture and cook about 3 to 5 minutes longer. Deglaze the pan with red wine, then add the stock and tomato sauce. Bring to a boil then reduce the heat and simmer for 15 to 20 minutes. Meanwhile, preheat the oven to 350 degrees.

Place shanks in a roasting pan and cover with the sauce. The shanks should be completely covered with the liquid. Put the small bouquet garni inside the pan, cover with aluminum foil and roast in a 350 degree oven for 3 hours.

While the shanks are cooking, soak the porcini mushrooms in boiling chicken broth, making sure that the mushrooms are completely covered, about 2 hours until soft. Strain the mushrooms, chop and set aside. Place the cooked shanks on a platter, strain the sauce from the roasting pan and put back on the stove in the same roasting pan. Add the glace de viande, chopped porcini mushrooms and lemon zest, cook over medium heat to warm the sauce through about 5 minutes. Check the seasoning and adjust if needed. Pour the sauce over the veal shanks and sprinkle with parsley.

Tomato Sauce

Makes 2½ cups

¼ cup olive oil

1 tablespoon minced garlic

1 stalk of celery, chopped

2 tablespoons carrots, chopped

1 small onion, chopped

2½ pounds ripened tomatoes, coarsely chopped

Heat the oil in a saucepan over medium-high heat, add the garlic, celery, carrots and onions. Sauté until soft, then add the tomatoes, lower the heat and let simmer for about 30 minutes. Remove from heat and set aside.

Veal Glace de Viande
Makes 2 cups

5 pounds veal shank end bones

1 pound veal breast, cut into 1-inch cubes

1 carrot, cut into 1-inch thick slices

1½ onions, cut into 1-inch cubes

1 celery stalk, cut into 1-inch pieces

2 tablespoons olive oil

Salt and pepper

1 gallon of water

2 sprigs fresh thyme

5 sprigs fresh parsley

1 bay leaf

2 garlic cloves

Put the veal bones, veal breast pieces and vegetables on a baking sheet. Rub the veal with olive oil, salt and pepper and place in a 400 degree oven for 1 hour or until very brown all over. Remove the baking sheet from the oven and place everything into a stock pot. Discard all the fat from the baking sheet and deglaze with water and then add this liquid to the stock pot. Add the remaining water, herbs and garlic to the stock pot and bring to a boil. Reduce the heat and simmer for about 8 hours.

When done, skim the fat off the top and then strain the stock. Place the stock in a container and chill overnight.

The next day, remove any hardened fat that has formed at the top. Place the stock back into a pot and bring to a rapid boil for 1 to 2 hours or until the stock reduces to 2 cups.

FENNEL ASPARAGUS RISOTTO

Makes 10 servings

¼ pound butter

½ cup carrots, finely diced

¼ cup shallots, finely diced

½ cup celery, finely diced

1 cup shaved fennel bulb

2 tablespoons garlic, minced

3 cups raw Arborio rice

½ bottle white wine

5 cups chicken broth, warmed

1 cup grated parmesan cheese

2½ cups asparagus tips, blanched

¾ cup shaved fennel, sautéed

¼ cup shaved parmesan cheese

Using a heavy duty pan over medium heat, melt 4 tablespoons butter and add the carrots, shallots, celery, fennel and garlic. Sauté until golden brown, about 7 minutes. Add the rice, stir and continue to cook until golden brown. Add the wine and deglaze the pan. Begin adding the warm chicken broth, one ladle at a time to the rice and stir occasionally until the liquid is absorbed. Continue this process until all the broth has been absorbed and the rice is cooked. Add the parmesan cheese and 4 tablespoons more butter to finish it off. Check the seasonings and adjust if needed.

Remove from the heat and fold in the blanched asparagus tips and sautéed shaved fennel to the risotto, top with shaved parmesan and serve.

GRILLED VEGETABLES

Makes 10 servings

2 pounds bell peppers, (yellow, green, and red)

2 pounds red onion

1 pound yellow zucchini

2 pounds green zucchini

1 pound red potatoes

2 pounds carrots

1 pound parsnips

2 pounds mushrooms

½ pound cherry tomatoes

1 pound asparagus or green beans

1 pound eggplant

4 cups Vegetable Marinade *(see recipe index)*

Slice the vegetables to your preference and marinate them in the Vegetable Marinade overnight in the refrigerator. The next day, grill all the vegetables except for the carrots, parsnips and potatoes. Take the carrots, parsnips and potatoes and roast them in oven at 375 degrees until they are brown, 30 to 45 minutes. When all of the vegetables are cooked, season with salt and pepper.

WHITE CHOCOLATE PANNA COTTA WITH BLUEBERRY GELATIN AND BLUEBERRY SYRUP
Makes 10 servings

Blueberry Gelatin

3 sheets gelatin
(available in specialty stores)

1 cup water (to soak the gelatin)

1¾ cups crème de cassis

½ cup sugar

1 to 2 baskets of blueberries, some are for the garnish

Soak the gelatin sheets in water in a small bowl and set aside. Boil the crème de cassis and sugar in a pot until sugar dissolves, about five minutes. Remove the pot from the heat and add the melted gelatin.

Prepare individual serving bowls by placing the desired amount of blueberries in the bottom of each bowl. Pour the gelatin over the blueberries and fill to about ¼-inch full, approximately 3 tablespoons for each dish. Place in the refrigerator and chill for five hours.

White Chocolate Panna Cotta

5 sheets gelatin
(available in specialty stores)

¼ cup milk

4 cups heavy cream

½ cup granulated sugar

1 vanilla bean, split and scraped

3½ ounces chopped white chocolate

Place the five sheets of gelatin in a small bowl, add the milk and allow to stand for 10 minutes. Put the cream, sugar and vanilla in a saucepan over medium heat and bring to a boil. Remove from the heat and add the gelatin mixture and whisk until it is dissolved. Add the chocolate and stir until it is melted and the mixture is smooth. Strain the mixture through a sieve. Take the bowls of the blueberry gelatin out of the refrigerator and pour the panna cotta mixture over the blueberry gelatin to fill the bowls. Refrigerate for 4 to 6 hours or until set.

Blueberry syrup
Makes ½ cup

½ cup water

½ cup crème de cassis

2 tablespoons sugar

Boil the water, crème de cassis and sugar in a small pot, stirring occasionally, and cooking until syrupy and reduced to about a ½ cup. This should take about 10 to 12 minutes. Set the syrup aside to chill.

To assemble the panna cotta, dip the bowls into hot water to loosen them. Then flip them over and out onto a plate. Drizzle the blueberry syrup around the panna cotta. Place a cookie and a biscotti *(recipes to follow)* next to the panna cotta layered on top of each other. Spoon some syrup onto the plate and sprinkle with some loose berries. You can use a rosemary stem as a skewer for some fresh blueberries to add an interesting twist.

CHOCOLATE CHIP CHRISTINE COOKIE
Makes 5 dozen cookies

¼ cup brown sugar

¼ cup white sugar

3 ounces butter

1 egg

½ teaspoon vanilla

¼ cup whole wheat flour

⅛ teaspoon baking powder

⅛ teaspoon salt

¼ teaspoon baking soda

¼ cup wheat germ

¼ cup mini chocolate chips

¼ cup walnut pieces (small)

¼ cup shredded coconut

In a kitchen mixer, cream together the brown sugar, white sugar and butter until light and fluffy. Add the egg and vanilla and beat well.

In a separate bowl, sift together the flour, baking powder, salt and baking soda. Add this into the sugar mixture, beating well. Scrape down the bowl and stir in the wheat germ, chocolate chips, walnuts and coconut.

Scoop measuring teaspoons of dough onto parchment lined baking pans. Place plastic wrap (to help keep the dough from sticking to your fingers) over the dough and flatten with your fingers to make very thin cookies.

Bake in a 375 degree oven for 5 to 6 minutes. Remove from the oven and cool the cookies on racks.

Store cookies in an air-tight container after they have cooled or the cookies will get soft.

HAZELNUT BISCOTTI
Makes 12 biscotti (4-inches each)

¼ cup brown sugar

1 egg

2 egg whites

¼ cup sugar

¾ cup all-purpose flour

⅛ teaspoon salt

⅛ teaspoon baking soda

⅓ cup hazelnuts

¼ tablespoon hazelnut liqueur

In a kitchen mixer, beat the brown sugar and 1 whole egg until thick, set aside. In a separate bowl, whip the egg whites and granulated sugar until very thick, set aside.

Sift together the flour, salt and baking soda. In a large bowl, combine the brown sugar mixture, egg white mixture and flour mixture together. Stir in the hazelnuts and liqueur, mixing well.

Lightly spray a baking pan with nonstick spray. Form the dough into two logs and place on the baking pan. Bake in a 300 degree oven for 15 minutes until golden brown. Remove from the oven and slice each log into finger size slices. Lay them back on the baking pan on their sides and put back into the oven, reducing the heat to 250 degrees and bake for about 45 minutes to 1 hour until crisp.

Sparkling Limoncello Martini

2 ounces Limoncello
4 ounces sparkling wine
Lemon slices for garnish
Lavender sprigs for garnish

Chill martini glasses, pour in Limoncello and sparkling wine, and garnish

How to make your own Limoncello

15 Meyer lemons
2 750ml bottles of 100 proof vodka
2 cups water
2 cups sugar

With a potato peeler, peel the lemon rinds into long strips, being careful not to get any of the white pith. Place lemon peels into a large container and add 1 bottle of vodka. Seal and let the container sit at room temperature for two weeks.

After the two weeks are up, make a simple syrup by heating the sugar and water over medium heat for five to seven minutes. Let the syrup cool completely. Then pour the syrup into the vodka lemon mixture. Add the second bottle of vodka, cover and let rest for an additional week at room temperature.

When the week is up, strain the mixture and place the limoncello in a glass bottle in the freezer until ready to serve. Serve in little chilled glasses, icy cold.

Entertainment and Musical Ambiance

Music and entertainment is another way you can express yourself and it certainly adds another element to your gathering. On this "Sunday Kind of Love" occasion we played light opera, embracing the sounds of the tenors. To give another dimension, consider hiring a musician, like a violist, who plays romantic Italian music or a classical guitarist. Having live music makes it very special. When selecting your music give it some status, don't just set up your iPod with a selection of music. Consider inviting people for dinner with the sounds of The Beatles, old standards or Broadway tunes - conversation always ensues.

Live entertainment also adds to the party. For a dinner I recently did for my husband's golf buddies and spouses, I arranged for a "Tiger Woods" lookalike to drop by. Corny, I know, but it certainly brought a smile and a photo opportunity for them all and a new energy to the dinner party.

When you have larger social occasions, I recommend you secure any entertainment needs through an entertainment broker. You can be sure they will get the best price, give you more choices that you may not even have thought of, help you make selections and make sure your entertainers have all the correct event details such as arriving on time, dressing correctly as well as having their equipment and sound needs met. Dealing directly with performers is not always the easiest. To have an expert who understands all these requirements, the personalities of your entertainers and your expectations for the event is precious and well worth the investment.

LIFE IS A BEACH
A *time to relax and enjoy*

I came to California 26 years ago from England with two children and a husband. I had the good fortune to live in Malibu which, although paradise, was certainly a total culture shock! Never having lived by the ocean, I loved waking up to the sight of the ocean and going to bed with the sound of the waves. The ocean became a part of our lives and we never took its beauty or power for granted. Truly, for us, life was the beach.

While the ocean became another family member, so did the friends we made by it. Two of those friends are Christine and Leo. Our children grew up together and we spent many hours enjoying each other's company on the beach.

We have since moved away from Malibu, whereas Leo and Christine still live there. Every now and again we gather to spend time at the beach with new friends and old. The children have now grown so it is always good to catch up and share.

We met at a local beach club in Malibu after Labor Day so that the beach could be our own. As we have all gotten a little older, somehow, spreading blankets on the sand was not as appealing as it used to be.

Instead, we created a table with a small fire pit set at the center. The fire added drama with the added benefit of warmth when the sun set. Beach balls strewn around the table added to the ambience and alluded back to the day when our children would spend hours playing on the beach. Back then we might have had peanut butter and jelly sandwiches but, this evening we dined on crab sliders followed by lobster and steak. Dessert was key lime cupcakes topped with meringue.

The fire came into play again as our unique centerpiece became the perfect place to make s'mores. This enchanted evening by the ocean is truly the reason I thank goodness that life is a beach.

Menu

Preview
Dungeness Crab Slider with Avocado

Old Bay Sprinkled Popcorn with Celery Leaf

Main
Grilled Lobster Tails with Basil Butter

Russet Potato with Chive and

Grainy Mustard Butter

Rustic White and Yellow Sweet Corn Flan

Grilled Rib Eye Steak with Mushrooms

Grilled Chayote Squash Gratin

Indulge
S'mores by the Camp fire

Key Lime Cupcakes

Libation
Elderberry Flower Margarita

DUNGENESS CRAB SLIDERS

Makes 22 sliders

2 tablespoons butter

½ cup shallots, minced

2 pounds fresh Dungeness crab meat

2 tablespoons chives

3 tablespoons lemon juice

1 tablespoon parsley

2 tablespoons mayonnaise

1 teaspoon Dijon mustard

1 tablespoon Worcestershire sauce

⅓ cup breadcrumbs

Cayenne pepper to taste

Salt and pepper to taste

2 tablespoons extra virgin olive oil

Slider Remoulade Sauce *(recipe to follow)*

22 mini burger buns

3 ripe avocados

22 3-inch bamboo skewers with knots

In a skillet, sauté the butter and shallots on medium heat until soft. Transfer to a bowl and set aside to cool. In a large bowl, mix the crab, chives, lemon juice, parsley, shallots, mayonnaise, Dijon mustard, Worcestershire sauce and breadcrumbs. Add cayenne pepper to taste and mix well. Season with salt and pepper. Place in the refrigerator and let sit for about 10 minutes to firm. Remove from the refrigerator and form 22 sliders by hand. Sear on a hot griddle or frying pan with a little olive oil for 2 minutes on each side, until golden brown.

To assemble, cut the buns in half and lay the crab slider (warmed or room temperature) on the bottom half of the bun. Cut the avocado in half and take out the seed. Scoop the avocado out of the skin. Thinly slice the avocado and lay about 4 slices on the top half of the burger bun. Place a large dollop of Slider Remoulade Sauce on the avocado and then place the top half of the bun over the crab cake and insert a skewer through the slider to hold it together and serve.

Slider Remoulade Sauce

Makes 2 cups

¼ cup pickle relish

¼ cup minced shallots (3 ounces)

2 tablespoons capers

½ teaspoon garlic, minced

1¼ cup mayonnaise

½ cup sour cream

Salt and white pepper to taste

Blend everything together in a food processor, leaving the sauce a little chunky. Adjust seasonings if needed.

OLD BAY SPRINKLED POPCORN WITH CELERY LEAF

Makes one medium bowl of popcorn

1 cup white popcorn

⅓ cup vegetable oil

2 tablespoons Old Bay seasoning

Salt and pepper to taste

Celery leaves off one bunch of celery

Parchment paper to make cones

Circular paper clips

Pour the oil into a heavy duty pot with a lid over high heat and wait a couple of minutes, then add the popcorn. Cover with the lid and shake the pot back and forth regularly while the popcorn is popping to stop it from burning and to make for a more even pop. When the popcorn stops popping, pour it into a bowl and add the Old Bay seasoning, salt, pepper and celery leaves and toss so that the seasonings are spread evenly over the popcorn.

Make a cone with the parchment paper and use the clip to hold the cone together. Fill it with popcorn, sprinkle with the celery leaves and serve.

GRILLED LOBSTER TAILS WITH BASIL BUTTER

Makes 10 portions

10 lobster tails in shells (8-10 ounces each)

2 cups Vegetable Marinade *(see recipe index)*

½ pound Basil Butter *(recipe to follow)*

Salt and pepper to taste

The day before, take the lobster tails and cut down the back of the lobster shell with scissors. Use your fingers to pull the meat away from the shell in one piece. Marinate the whole tails in the vegetable marinade overnight. To cook, heat up the grill and cook the tails over medium heat for about 10 minutes, rotating them so that they cook evenly. Cut the tails in half lengthwise, place a slice of Basil Butter on top and serve.

Basil Butter

½ pound butter softened

1 ounce basil, chiffonade

Put the softened butter into a bowl and fold in the chiffonade of basil. When it is mixed together evenly, place the butter on a piece of parchment or plastic wrap and form a log in the size and thickness you want. Roll it up in plastic wrap and place in the refrigerator to firm. When the butter is firm, slice it to your desired thickness.

RUSSET POTATOES WITH CHIVE AND GRAINY MUSTARD BUTTER

Makes 10 potatoes

10 large russet potatoes

½ cup olive oil

Salt and pepper to taste

1 cup sour cream

½ pound butter

¾ cup nine grain mustard

Clean the potatoes with cold water. Pierce the potatoes with the tines of a fork in about 4 or 5 places around the potato and rub lightly with olive oil, salt and pepper then wrap in foil. You can par bake the potatoes in a 350 degree oven for 40 minutes and then bake them off on the grill for 20 minutes. Or, you can cook them just on the grill for about 60 minutes, rotating occasionally. When that potatoes are cooked, cut an 'X' on top of each potato and squeeze the potato so that it opens up. Garnish with your choice of a combination of sour cream, butter or nine grain mustard.

RUSTIC YELLOW AND WHITE SWEET CORN FLAN

Makes 10 servings

1 cup chicken broth

1¼ cups heavy cream

5 ears yellow corn, cut the kernels off the cob, save both

5 ears white corn, whole

1 tablespoon thyme

¼ cup carrot, diced

¼ cup white onion, diced

¼ cup of celery, diced

2 teaspoons roasted garlic

2 cups canned creamed corn

7 eggs

Put chicken broth, ¾ cup of cream, 3 yellow corn cobs and thyme in a pot and bring to a boil. Lower the heat and simmer for 10 minutes to allow flavors to infuse. Strain, discard the corn cobs and thyme and reserve the liquid.

Sauté the carrots, onions, celery, roasted garlic and yellow corn kernels in a pan for 10 minutes with salt and pepper until cooked through.

In a blender or food processor, blend the reserved liquid and the sautéed corn mixture. Add the creamed corn, eggs and ½ cup of cream until it is all puréed. Strain the mixture through a sieve or food mill, place it in a container and set aside. Throw away all the left over corn and vegetables that were caught in the strainer.

Grill the 5 ears of white corn over a hot grill for 5 minutes until golden brown. When they are cool enough to handle, cut the kernels off the cob. To assemble the flan, fill 10 individual 4-ounce dishes ¼ full with the grilled corn kernels and top with the flan mixture until almost full to the top. Place the filled dishes in a pan filled half way with hot water (to create a water bath) and bake in a 350 degree oven for 20 minutes until the flans becomes firm. Remove the pan from oven.

To serve, turn the dishes upside down to unmold the flan onto a plate. Garnish with grilled white corn kernels.

GRILLED RIB EYE STEAK WITH MUSHROOMS

Makes 10 steaks and 6 cups mushrooms

10 rib eye steaks, 1-inch thick

½ cup olive oil

Salt and pepper to taste

½ pound butter

1 pound portabello mushrooms, cut into 16 wedges

1 pound cremini mushrooms, cut in half if large

½ pound chanterelle mushrooms, cut in half if large

½ pound oyster mushrooms, cut in half if large

¼ cup Glace de Viande *(see recipe index)*

Season the steaks with salt and pepper and rub with a little olive oil. Place the steaks onto a hot grill for 3 to 5 minutes on each side. Remove steaks from the grill and let them rest a few minutes.

In a nice hot pan with some butter and oil, sauté the mushrooms for about 10 minutes to a golden brown. Sprinkle the mushrooms with salt and pepper and toss in a small amount of Glace de Viande to lightly coat the mushrooms. Spoon a portion of the mushrooms on top of each grilled steak and serve.

GRILLED CHAYOTE SQUASH GRATIN

Makes 10 servings

5 chayote squash

½ cup Vegetable Marinade *(see recipe index)*

16 ounces ricotta cheese

2 cups toasted bread crumbs

1 cup grated parmesan cheese

¼ cup parsley, chopped

2 tablespoons garlic, minced

1 tablespoon salt

1 teaspoon pepper

The day before, cut the chayotes in half and scoop out the seeds. Marinate in the Vegetable Marinade overnight.

To prepare, grill the chayotes on a high heat until the color deepens. Remove from the grill and then place in a 350 degree oven and bake for 10 minutes to soften the chayotes and warm them through. Remove from the oven and spread one tablespoon of ricotta cheese on the inside of each one.

In a bowl, mix together the remaining ingredients. Sprinkle a good portion of this topping over the chayote. Place the squash under broiler and cook 3 to 5 minutes until golden brown and serve.

KEY LIME CUPCAKES
Makes 16 medium cupcakes

½ cup unsalted butter, room temperature

1¼ cups sugar

1 large egg

2½ tablespoons fresh lime juice

1 tablespoon finely grated lime peel

¼ teaspoon neon green food coloring

1 cup all-purpose flour, sifted

¾ cup cake flour, sifted

1½ teaspoons baking powder

¾ cup buttermilk

Lime Curd *(recipe to follow)*

Swiss Meringue *(recipe to follow)*

Candied Lime Zest *(recipe to follow)*

Preheat the oven to 350 degrees. Line standard muffin pans with paper liners. Beat the butter in a kitchen mixer with the paddle attachment until soft and creamy, then add the sugar and beat until light and fluffy. Add the egg and beat well. Add the lime juice, lime peel and food coloring and continue to beat.

Sift all dry ingredients together into a bowl and then add them along with the buttermilk to the batter, alternating between the two. Scoop the batter into the paper liners. Bake for 10 minutes and then remove from the oven. Put the Lime Curd in a piping bag and pipe a teaspoon of it into the middle of the cupcake, just beneath the top layer. Be careful not to pipe too far into the middle of the cupcake. Put the cupcakes back into the oven and bake for 10 to 15 minutes longer until a toothpick inserted into the cakes comes out clean.

When cooled, frost the cupcakes with the Swiss Meringue and use a kitchen blow torch to burn the edges to a nice golden brown. Sprinkle with Candied Lime Zest.

Candied Lime Zest
Makes ½ cup

5 limes

1 cup granulated sugar + 1 cup to toss

¾ cup water

Make long strips of zest by using the large holes on a grater and scraping along the limes from top to bottom, set aside. Put the water and sugar in a pot over low heat to dissolve the sugar. Once the sugar has dissolved, bring up to a boil and add the lime zest. Boil for about 10 minutes until the zest is soft. Strain the lime zest out and toss it in 1 cup of granulated sugar to coat. Spread the sugar-coated zest out on a sheet pan and let sit for about 30 minutes to soak up the sugar. When the 30 minutes is up, toss in sugar again, adding more sugar if needed. Strain the zest from the sugar and let them sit out to dry, about 2 hours.

Lime Curd
Makes ¾ cup (put about 1 teaspoon in each cupcake)

4 egg yolks, lightly beaten

½ cup granulated sugar

⅓ cup fresh key lime juice

2¼ teaspoons grated lime rind

In the top of a double boiler, combine the egg yolks, sugar, and lime juice. Cook the mixture over moderate heat for about 10 minutes, until it coats the back of a spoon. Remove from the heat and stir in the grated lime rind. Chill until the mixture thickens.

Swiss Meringue
Makes 4 cups

4 large egg whites

1 cup sugar

Pinch cream of tartar

½ teaspoon vanilla extract

Fill a medium saucepan ¼ full with water. Set over low heat and bring the water to a light simmer. Mix the egg whites, sugar and cream of tartar in a metal bowl with an electric mixer until foamy and then place the bowl over the simmering saucepan. Whisk constantly by hand until the sugar is dissolved and it is warm to the touch, about 3 minutes.

Rub the mixture between your fingers to test that the sugar has dissolved and it is not grainy. Remove the bowl from the heat and whip, starting on low speed and gradually increasing to high speed, until the meringue is cool and stiff glossy peaks form, about 10 minutes. Add the vanilla and mix until it is combined. Use immediately.

BANANA S'MORES BY THE CAMP FIRE

Banana bread *(recipe to follow)* or graham crackers

Homemade marshmallows *(recipe to follow)*

Hershey chocolate bars

Fresh bananas

Metal skewers

Arrange banana bread slices, marshmallow and chocolate squares on a platter. Peel and slice fresh bananas on the diagonal to create some different shapes and place the slices on the platter next to the banana bread slices. Last but not least, add the metal skewer to the platter for toasting the marshmallows.

Banana Bread
Makes 1 loaf

6 ripe bananas

2 eggs

⅓ cup vegetable oil

1 cup granulated sugar

1½ teaspoons vanilla

1¾ cups all-purpose flour

1½ teaspoons baking powder

1½ teaspoons baking soda

¼ teaspoon salt

Mash the bananas in a bowl and set aside. In a separate bowl, whisk together the eggs, oil, sugar and vanilla and add this to the mashed banana. Sift the flour, baking powder, baking soda and salt together and fold into the banana mixture. Spray an 11¼ x 4¼-inch loaf pan with cooking spray and fill it ¾ full with the batter. Bake in a 350 degree oven for 30 minutes, turn the heat down to 325 degrees and bake approximately 30 minutes longer until done.

Once cooled, cut it down the middle lengthwise and slice it into ¼-inch slices.

Marshmallows

Makes a 9x12-inch sheet pan

1¼ cups cornstarch

⅓ cup confectioners sugar

1 envelope unflavored gelatin (1 heaping tablespoon)

⅓ cup cold water

⅔ cup granulated sugar

½ cup light corn syrup

Pinch of salt

1 teaspoon vanilla extract

Sift the cornstarch and confectioners sugar together into a bowl. Lightly grease a 9x12-inch square baking sheet and sprinkle one tablespoon of the cornstarch and sugar mixture into it. Tilt the pan to coat the sides and the bottom and leave any excess in the pan.

Put the water into a small saucepan and sprinkle the gelatin in and let soak for 5 minutes. Add the granulated sugar to the gelatin and place over low heat, stirring until the gelatin and sugar dissolve. In a large bowl, combine the gelatin mixture, corn syrup, salt and vanilla and whisk with a mixer for 15 minutes on high speed, until peaks form. Spread the fluffy mixture in the prepared pan and smooth the top. Leave for 2 hours or until set.

With a wet knife, cut the marshmallow into quarters and loosen around the edges. Sprinkle the remaining cornstarch and sugar mixture on a baking sheet and invert the marshmallow blocks onto it. Cut each quarter into 9 pieces and roll each one in the cornstarch and sugar mixture again.

Place the marshmallow squares on a cake rack and cover with paper towels. Let them stand over night so that the surface dries. The marshmallow squares will keep for up to a month if stored in airtight containers.

Elderberry Flower Margarita

2 ounces tequila

2 ounces elderberry flower juice *(found at Swedish specialty stores)*

2 ounces ruby red grapefruit juice

Splash of Cointreau

Pour all ingredients over ice and serve.

Greening Your Event Serviceware

The philosophy of creating a totally green event looks great on paper (recycled of course!) but in practice it can be complicated. From what we've found in our research into serviceware, many landfills are not yet ready to take on bio-degradable products such as plates made from potato or bamboo. In simple terms, these products need light and air to degrade and many landfills are enclosed. On the other side of the coin, there are recycling systems in place for certain plastics. So, not all plastics are a bad thing. Acrylic products, though they cost a little more, are really great looking and can be recycled. China and glassware are wonderful options also because they are reusable. Creating an eco-friendly event is certainly possible but some decisions have to be made about how to proceed. I suggest looking at your event – how it will be set up, where it will take place, what type of feeling you are trying to create, etc. – before determining what type of plates and flatware will work for you.

Cheating at the Grill

The art of grilling is a talent. There is a 'trick of the trade' though when grilling for a crowd. Par (or pre) roast your chicken, beef or lobster. Doing so begins the cooking process so that your meat will be grilled in half the time and won't burn on the outside. When you bring the par-cooked meat to a really hot grill, you will be able to get those perfect grill marks and seal in the flavors of the meat without fear of over-cooking.

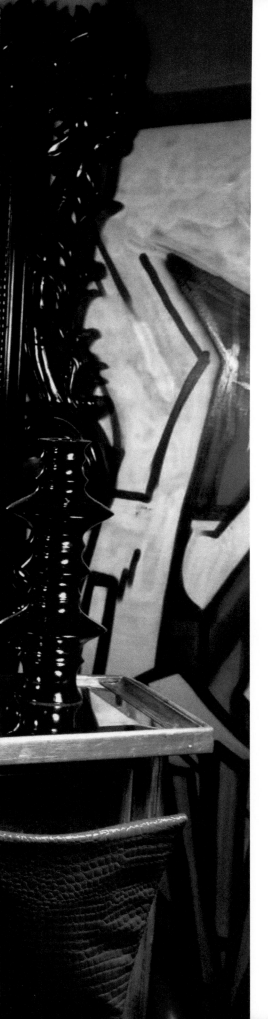

CITY WAREHOUSE
After-hours indulgence

There are certain parties for which the entire look and feel hinges around the location. While not everyone can boast a 30,000-square-foot warehouse, like the one that event designer Rrivre Davies owns, there are downtown loft spaces and warehouses available for party rentals in almost every city.

The warehouse/downtown party has become a classic. Normally they are austere, arty affairs with concrete floors and barren walls. Not in this case. Not at all! As owner of Rrivre Works, one of Los Angeles' top event design companies and prop houses, Rrivre has stuffed his warehouse to the rafters with glorious, custom-made props — unique chandeliers, tables, bars, furniture, and more. It was the perfect setting for an after-hours party for family, friends and colleagues.

The event did not even start until 11 pm and although that is a little past my bedtime, I am always up for a celebration of food, fun and love, no matter what the hour! Plus, I knew my staff would embrace this kind of event.

We centered the party in one specific area of the massive warehouse, capturing many of the decorative details with some graffiti artwork woven through the environment. Thanks to Rrive, we didn't need to set up any additional equipment or props, merely enhance what was already in place. A DJ spun ultra-hip house music (what, no Michael Buble?!) and we served indulgent comfort food that was more along the lines of a snacky breakfast you might have if you were raiding the fridge at two in the morning. We also presented a sustainable American caviar bar, a bit of frivolity that was met with much appreciation.

We passed food on silver sparkly trays to give the event a glam feeling. The staff wore black T-shirts with tattoo arm "stockings," leather wrist bands and fedora hats that made them look a bit edgy. The favorite martini of the night was pear vodka with white cranberry juice and a splash of ruby red grapefruit dressed up with an edible hibiscus. After all, these kids have to get their daily allotment of veggies, fruit and flowers somehow! Needless to say, I don't believe anyone made it out of bed before noon the next morning.

Now that's living like a downtown artist!

Menu

Preview
Pork Apple Sausage Burger
pickled red cabbage and apple mustard
on a petite bun

Lacquered Chicken and Waffles
rosemary maple syrup

Falafel Pizza
yogurt mint sauce with cucumber

Grit Sticks wrapped in Prosciutto
secret sauce in black and white boxes

Indulge
French Toast Cubes with Nutella Cream

Triple Berry Smoothies
caramel nut clusters

Main
Pumpkin Seed Chicken Caesar Soy Cone
balsamic caesar dressing

Best-Ever Egg Salad Sandwich
with smoked salmon, capers, dill,
red onions, green olives and tomatoes

Frisée Pancetta Salad
tossed with mustard dressing in egg shells
topped with fried quail eggs

Sustainable Infused Caviars
beet and saffron, ginger and truffle
served with toasts

Libation
Rrivretini
pear vodka with grapefruit juice
served with edible hybiscus

PORK APPLE SAUSAGE BURGERS
Makes 20 burgers

4 apples

2 tablespoons butter

2 cups sugar

2 pounds ground pork or sausage meat (1½ ounces per burger)

Salt and pepper to taste

2 cups Sautéed Red Cabbage with Balsamic Vinegar *(recipe to follow)*

1 cup Apple Mustard Sauce *(recipe to follow)*

20 mini burger buns

Peel and core the apples and cut into small cubes. Caramelize the apples in butter and sugar in a sauté pan over medium heat for about 10 minutes until soft and brown, remove and set aside to cool. When the apples are cooled, fold into the pork meat and add the salt and pepper. Mold the pork mixture into 20 mini burgers and set aside until ready to cook. Make the red cabbage sauté and apple mustard and set aside.

When you are ready to serve, grill the burgers over a high heat for about 5 minutes on each side until completely cooked and set on paper towels to drain any oil. Cut the burger buns in half through the middle. Spread the top half of the bun with the apple mustard sauce and place the grilled burger on the bottom half of the bun. Put a spoonful of the warm cabbage sauté on the burger, add the top of the bun and serve.

Sautéed Red Cabbage with Balsamic Vinegar
Makes 2 cups

2 tablespoons unsalted butter

½ head red cabbage, shredded

2 tablespoons balsamic vinegar

⅓ cup chicken stock

Salt and pepper to taste

Melt the butter in a pan over medium heat. Add the cabbage and vinegar, stirring occasionally, until softened, 5 to 7 minutes. Add the stock, turn the heat down to low, and cook covered for 20 minutes or until it is soft.

Apple Mustard Sauce
Makes 1 cup

¾ cups canned apples, with their juice

2 tablespoons sugar

1 teaspoon lemon juice

½ cup Dijon mustard

Cook the canned apples with the juice, sugar and lemon juice together over medium heat, stirring occasionally for approximately 30 minutes. When apples are thickened, mash in the pan with a potato masher. Continue cooking, stirring frequently, until the sauce becomes mostly dry. Set aside to chill. Once cooled, puree the apples in a food processor and add the Dijon mustard.

LACQUERED CHICKEN AND WAFFLES WITH ROSEMARY MAPLE DRIZZLE

Makes 20 pieces

20 Lacquered Chicken Drumettes *(recipe to follow)*

20 mini Eggo® waffles *(store bought)*

1 cup Rosemary Maple Syup *(recipe to follow)*

1 bunch rosemary for garnish

Toast the waffles and place the warmed Lacquered Chicken Drumettes on top of the waffles. Drizzle with some of the Rosemary Maple Syrup, garnish with a little sprig of rosemary and serve.

Lacquered Chicken Drumettes
Makes 20 drumettes

20 small chicken drumettes (drumsticks)

2 cups soy sauce

2 cups granulated white sugar

2 teaspoons powdered ginger

2 tablespoons garlic powder

½ cup red wine vinegar

Mix all the ingredients except for the drumettes in a bowl to make the marinade. Take out 2 cups of the marinade and reserve for use later. Add the chicken drumettes into the bowl and toss, then place in the refrigerator overnight.

To cook, place the chicken with the marinade on a sheet pan and place in a 350 degree oven and bake for 20 minutes until the chicken is cooked. Remove from the oven and pour off the excess juices. Add the reserved 2 cups of marinade to the chicken and place the sheet pan on the stove top and cook over a medium high heat, rotating the chicken constantly, for about 20 minutes until the marinade is reduced to a sticky glaze.

Rosemary Maple Syrup
Makes ½ cup

½ cup maple syrup

1 sprig of rosemary

In a saucepan, bring the maple syrup and rosemary to a boil. After it comes to a boil, turn the heat down and simmer for 5 to10 minutes so the syrup becomes infused with rosemary.

FALAFEL PIZZA
Makes 20 pizzas

5 9x12-inch flat breads, cut into 4 squares

¾ cup butter garlic olive oil mixture *(see recipe index)*

¾ cup cream cheese

⅓ cup tahini

Salt and pepper to taste

2 tablespoons roasted garlic (to taste)

20 Falafel balls, torn in small pieces *(recipe to follow)*

1⅔ cups red bell pepper, julienne

1¼ red onions, cut in a medium dice and caramelized

1⅔ cups kalamata olives, each cut lengthwise into four slices

¼ cup flat leaf parsley, chopped

1 cup Yogurt Mint Sauce with Cucumber *(recipe to follow)*

Brush the flatbread with the butter garlic olive oil mixture. Toast in the oven at 325 degrees for 7 minutes until golden brown and crisp. Make the tahini spread by beating the cream cheese in the mixer with the tahini paste and sprinkle with salt, pepper and roasted garlic to taste.

When the flatbread has cooled, spread with the tahini spread over the entire pizza. Sprinkle the torn falafel pieces, red bell pepper, caramelized onions and olives over the pizza. For the last touch, sprinkle with a little parsley. Drizzle the entire pizza with the yogurt mint sauce. Cut into squares and serve.

Falafel Balls
Makes 20 balls

1 can or 20 ounces of chick peas, drained

⅓ cup chives, chopped

⅓ cup mint leaves, chopped

2 teaspoons garlic, minced

½ teaspoon ground cumin

½ teaspoon ground coriander

1 tablespoon finely grated lemon rind

¾ teaspoon baking powder

2 tablespoons all-purpose flour

Sea salt and cracked black pepper to taste

½ cup egg whites

½ cup sesame seeds

Place the chick peas, chives, mint, garlic, cumin, coriander, lemon rind, baking powder, flour, salt and pepper in a food processor and process until smooth. Mold into little balls. Toss the balls lightly in additional flour, dip into the egg whites and then into the sesame seeds. Deep fry until golden brown. Drain on paper towels and let cool. When cooled, tear the balls into small pieces to add to the pizza.

GRITS STICKS WRAPPED IN PROSCIUTTO
Makes 30 sticks, 2x½-inch wide

Cheese Grits

2½ cups whole milk

2½ cups heavy cream

5 cups chicken broth

1 tablespoon salt

½ tablespoon white pepper

2 pounds white quick grits

1¼ pounds shredded white cheddar cheese

10 prosciutto slices, each cut into 3 strips

1 cup cornmeal

Hot oil for frying

Sauce

2 cups secret sauce (equal parts mayonnaise, mustard and ketchup)

1 cup ranch dressing

1½ tablespoons Tabasco

¼ cup cilantro, chopped

In a heavy duty pot over high heat, mix the milk, cream, chicken broth, salt and white pepper. Whisk until the mixture comes to a boil. Add the grits, reduce to medium heat and cook for about 1 hour, stirring frequently until cooked. Transfer to a bowl and slowly add in the white cheddar cheese, mixing with an electric mixer to blend. Spread the grits mixture evenly on a baking sheet covered with parchment paper and cover with more parchment paper. Put in the refrigerator until cooled.

While the cheesy grits are chilling, cut the prosciutto slices into 3 strips lengthwise and set aside. Prepare the sauce by mixing the secret sauce, ranch dressing and Tabasco together. Fold the cilantro into the sauce and set aside.

Cut the cheesy grits into stick shapes, 2 inches long by ½-inch wide. Roll the cheesy grits sticks in cornmeal, wrap one strip of prosciutto around each of the sticks and place in hot oil to fry until golden brown and crispy. Serve with the sauce on the side or piped right onto the sticks.

Yogurt Mint Sauce with Cucumber
Makes 1 cup

¾ cup yogurt

1 tablespoon lemon juice

1 tablespoon chopped mint

¼ cup grated cucumber

Pinch ground cumin

Pinch ground coriander

Pinch ground chili pepper

Salt and pepper to taste

Mix all the ingredients together in a small bowl. Check seasonings and adjust as needed.

CHICKEN CAESAR SALAD CONES

Makes 20 cones

2 chicken breasts

2 cups Balsamic Caesar Dressing *(recipe to follow)*

1–2 heads hearts of romaine lettuce

½ cup pumpkin seeds, toasted

5 sheets soy paper, any color *(available at Japanese markets or online at www.jfc.com)*

½ cup shredded parmesan cheese

The day before, clean and marinate the chicken breast in a ½ cup of Balsamic Caesar Dressing overnight. The next day, sear and cook the chicken in a 350 degree oven for 10 minutes or until the chicken is done. Let cool, then cut the chicken into a small dice. Cut the romaine lettuce into very small pieces, set aside. Spread the pumpkin seeds out on a cookie sheet, place in the oven at 350 degrees and toast until golden brown, about 5 to 7 minutes. Take out the toasted pumpkin seeds and set aside. Cut each soy paper sheet into 4 triangles and roll to form cones, set aside. You can make a holder for the cones by cutting 1½-inch holes in a piece of cardboard and slightly elevating it to allow the cones to sit inside. In a bowl, toss the chopped chicken, shredded romaine, toasted pumpkin seeds and parmesan with the remaining Balsamic Caesar Dressing. After this has been thoroughly tossed, place a small handful in each cone and sprinkle a little more of the pumpkin seeds on top as garnish. Serve immediately.

Balsamic Ceasar Dressing
Makes 2 cups

1 tablespoon balsamic vinegar

1 anchovy

1 tablespoon Dijon mustard

1½ teaspoons garlic, minced

1½ tablespoons Worcestershire sauce

1½ tablespoons lemon juice

2 eggs

1½ cups olive oil

¼ cup grated parmesan cheese

Ground black pepper to taste

Blend everything except olive oil and parmesan in a blender. Slowly add the olive oil into the blender, while it is running, until it emulsifies. Fold the parmesan into the dressing and season with pepper to taste.

BEST-EVER EGG SALAD SANDWICH WITH SMOKED SALMON

Makes 5 cups egg mixture, use ½ cup of mix per sandwich to make 10 whole sandwiches

1 cup green olives with pimento, chopped

¼ cup dill, sprigs removed from stem

1 cup red onions, diced

¼ cup capers, chopped

1½ cups tomatoes, peeled, seeded and chopped (about 5 tomatoes)

¾ cup Egg Salad Dressing *(recipe to follow)*

15 hard boiled eggs, each one cut into 8 pieces (use more egg white than yolks)

1 loaf brown bread, Pullman style, sliced thin, 20 slices

1½ pounds smoked salmon

Mix the olives, dill, red onion, capers and tomatoes in a bowl and lightly toss with ½ cup dressing. Mix the eggs in a separate bowl with the Egg Salad Dressing and fold lightly into the mixture. Adjust the seasonings as needed.

Lay the bread on a flat surface and place a slice of salmon on both sides of the sandwich. Put ½ cup of egg mixture onto the salmon on one side of the sandwich and lay the other half on top. Grill the sandwiches on a griddle or panini maker that has been sprayed with non-stick spray (do not put butter to the outside of the bread). Remove the crusts and cut each sandwich into four triangles and serve.

Egg Salad Dressing
Makes ¾ cup

½ cup mayonnaise

2 tablespoons Dijon mustard

1½ teaspoons roasted garlic

1½ teaspoons lemon juice

1½ teaspoons sugar

1 pinch cayenne

Pinch salt and pepper

Mix all the ingredients together in a bowl with a whisk. Check the seasonings and adjust as needed. This dressing can be made a day ahead and refrigerated.

FRISSÉE PANCETTA SALAD WITH MUSTARD DRESSING IN EGG SHELLS TOPPED WITH FRIED QUAIL EGG

Makes 10 servings

10 hard-boiled eggs

¼ pound pancetta, cut into a small dice

1 head of baby frisée

¼ cup Champagne Mustard Dressing *(recipe to follow)*

Salt and pepper to taste

10 quail eggs, gently fried

Oil for frying

To cook a hard-boiled egg perfectly, place a pot of water with a sprinkle of salt in it on the stove over high heat. When the water comes to a rapid boil, place the room temperature eggs slowly and carefully into the boiling water. When the water comes back to a boil, cook for 11 more minutes. Pour the hot water out of the pan and flush the eggs with cold water until the eggs are cold. This process makes for easy peeling and keeps the eggs from turning a grey color.

Take the un-peeled boiled eggs, cut the tops off and very carefully scoop the egg out of the shell leaving some egg white around the inside of the shell, then set side. Meanwhile, roast the pancetta in the oven at 350 degrees for 25 minutes. Strain off the extra fat and place the pancetta on paper towels to drain and cool. Cut the frisée into 2-inch pieces and place in a bowl with the chopped pancetta, dressing, salt and pepper. Toss well and fill the prepared egg shells with the salad.

Place a sauté pan on the stove over medium to high heat with a little oil. Crack a quail egg into the pan and gently use a spatula to flick the hot oil over the quail egg to cook the top. When the egg is fully cooked with semi-hard yolks, take it out of the pan and lay it on a paper towel to drain the oil. Repeat with all 10 quail eggs. Place one fried egg on the top of each of the frisée salad stuffed eggs and serve.

Champagne Mustard Dressing
Makes ¾ cups

1 tablespoon Dijon mustard

¼ cup champagne vinegar

1 teaspoon garlic, minced

½ cup olive oil

Salt and pepper to taste

Blend all the ingredients, except the oil, in a food processor. Slowly add the olive oil to the blender until the mixture emulsifies. Add salt and pepper to taste.

THREE CAVIARS AND TOAST

Three Caviars

American sustainable whitefish roe infused with beet and saffron

American sustainable whitefish roe infused with truffle

American sustainable whitefish roe infused with ginger

Served with toasts made from ficelle baguettes and sour cream garnish.

Ficelle Baguette Toasts
Makes approximately 48 toasts

2 Ficelle baguettes, sliced in ¼-inch slices

2 cups of olive oil

¼ pound butter

2 tablespoons minced garlic

Salt and pepper to taste

Put the olive oil, butter and garlic in a pot and bring to a boil. Remove from the heat and skim the foam off the top. Take the ficelle bread slices and dip, one side only, into the butter garlic olive oil mixture. Place the slices on a baking pan, oiled side up, and sprinkle with salt and pepper. Place in a 300 degree oven and bake for 10 minutes until the bread is hard to the touch. Set aside to cool.

FRENCH TOAST CUBES WITH NUTELLA CREAM
Makes 20 french toast cubes

2 cups heavy cream

6 eggs, beaten

1 tablespoon brandy

1½ tablespoons triple sec

¼ cup dark brown sugar

½ teaspoon cinnamon

½ teaspoon nutmeg

1 loaf of egg bread cut into 20 1½-inch cubes

Butter for frying

1 jar Nutella spread

2 cups whipped cream

1 cup tiny chocolate chips

The day before, combine the heavy cream, beaten eggs, brandy, triple sec, brown sugar, cinnamon and nutmeg in a large bowl and let this sit, covered, in the refrigerator for at least 6 hours or overnight. Place the bread cubes in a single layer on a cookie sheet. Pour the prepared liquid over the bread cubes until they are completely covered. Make sure to turn the bread so that it is well saturated throughout with the mixture. Cover the cubes with plastic wrap and let them soak for 2 hours, keep turning the bread occasionally to make sure that the mixture soaks in evenly.

Melt butter in a large skillet over medium heat, place the bread cubes in the pan and sauté them until they are lightly browned, about 30 seconds per side. Make sure that you turn the cubes so that all sides are browned. Transfer the bread cubes onto a cookie sheet and bake in a preheated oven at 350 degrees for around 10 minutes or until nice and puffy. To serve, make a little hole in each bread cube and fill with 1 teaspoon of Nutella. Pipe the whipped cream on top of each cube and sprinkle with tiny chocolate chips. Place on a tray and serve.

TRIPLE BERRY SMOOTHIES WITH CARAMEL NUT CLUSTERS

Makes 24 individual shot glass servings,
1-ounce each

1 cup mixed berries
(strawberries, blueberries, raspberries, blackberries)

½ cup non fat yogurt

1½ cups milk

24 caramel nut clusters *(recipe to follow)*

Mix the berries, milk and yogurt in a blender until you get a smooth consistency. Pour into a serving glass and garnish with a caramel nut cluster.

Caramel Nut Clusters
Makes 4 cups

1 tablespoon oil

¼ cup popcorn kernels (3 cups popped popcorn)

⅓ cup roasted peanuts

⅓ cup raw oats

½ cup granulated sugar

2 tablespoons water

2 teaspoons unsulfured dark molasses

1 tablespoon honey

1 tablespoon unsalted butter

¼ teaspoon baking soda

In a heavy duty pan heat the oil and popcorn kernels, cover with a lid and heat on medium-high until it starts to pop. Shake the pot carefully and keep shaking until the popping stops. In large bowl, mix together the popcorn, peanuts and oats (add a pinch of salt if you used unsalted peanuts). In another large saucepan, combine the sugar, water, molasses, honey and butter and stir once or twice. Clip a candy thermometer onto the side of the pan and place over medium to high heat. Bring to a boil and cook, without stirring, for 7 to 9 minutes or until the mixture registers 250 degrees on the thermometer. Remove the pan from the heat and add the baking soda. The mixture will foam up and then the foam will recede. Whisk just once, and then count off 5 seconds. Pour the mixture over the popcorn and peanuts and toss to distribute evenly. Be careful not to burn yourself!

Turn the mixture out onto a sheet pan that has been sprayed with non-stick spray and is covered with parchment paper. Using a heat-proof spatula, gently spread the popcorn mixture evenly on the pan. Let it cool to room temperature and then break it up into small clusters. The clusters will keep in an airtight container or covered with plastic wrap for 3 days.

How to determine food quantities

A common question we hear from clients is "how do we determine the amount of food we will need for an event?" One thing I tell them is that, as a caterer, I always allow for more than is needed – it's a cardinal sin for the caterer to run out of food. And it's the same for a host or hostess. There is just simply nothing worse. So, my advice to you when you are hosting a party is to allow for six bites of food per person per hour for cocktail parties.

If you have a buffet serving beef, fish and chicken, allow approximately 3 ounces per person per item – not full size portions. And if you are serving only chicken and fish, allow 4 ounces per person per item. A full portion is basically regarded as 8 ounces. If you have a selection of desserts allow for 4 small pieces per person. If you have 2 full size desserts, your guests will probably want a tasting of both so the rule is to allow for guests to have both but in smaller portions.

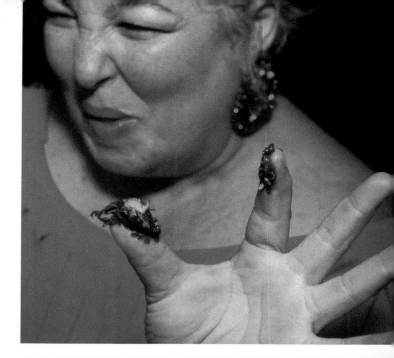

Location, location, location

You know the old saying is – success lies in the location. It's true for restaurants and it's true for parties. Not all homes can accommodate all types of parties, nor should they. Sometimes the style of an event is determined by the location. There are, of course, hotels that can host your party but, with so many fabulous off-premise caterers available today, the world is your oyster.

For instance, a location such as a museum can add so much if you are throwing an elegant event. I love the events that take place in the Natural History Museum here in Los Angeles. In fact, I had my own 50th birthday party in the glorious atrium of this museum. But, for more casual or themed events, consider parks, theaters, lofts or libraries. Often, when you throw an event in one of these spaces, you will find that your invitation becomes even more coveted; people are intrigued by the idea of coming together in different locales. The energy, ambience and built-in decor of these sites will lend much to your party. And yes, there may be some restrictions of one form or other but many of these sites are eager to hold events and allow you enough control to make the event your own.

LOVE THAT!
A glimpse back in time

Although they are famous for not divulging their ages, even movie stars like a birthday party. Virginia Madsen is no exception. A life-long friend of Jean Campbell, one of our event planners, Virginia calls on Jean and Good Gracious! when she wants to celebrate. A planner's dream, she is always open to new ideas. So, we presented her with some looks that would inspire her to go into a totally new direction from her previous parties.

The first look that Jean and I presented was retro-modern with a stylized wild color palette based on the Sixties. We also showed her two other story boards with more muted color palettes. To our surprise, and delight, she chose the retro Sixties look. We wasted no time in making it happen.

White lounge furniture was accented with bright yellow patent-leather chairs. Gerber daisies were used liberally. We created a pavé look with them by securing hundreds of them to Styrofoam pads with pearl headed pins. We carried the same design through with the birthday cake by placing Gerber daisies at the base of the cake. And, we added what I think will be the replacement for the ever-present cupcake - French macarons in pink and yellow to match the party. Daisies, inside Hula Hoops, even floated in the pool and were used to trim the lamps.

Guests were greeted with the signature drink of the evening, the Mad "V" Martini, before they dug into retro-based appetizers. We even dressed the staff in Bermuda shorts and orange polo shirts to match this period of time.

While the theme of Virginia's party made us all say "Groovy Baby" for days and weeks after, the blast to the past was worth it. Virginia is already looking forward to turning one year older just so she can see what we come up with next year!

Menu

Preview

Scallop Lemon Grass
grilled fresh scallops scented with
lightly curried lemon grass served on sugar cane

Mac and Cheese Cupcake
creamy macaroni cheddar cheese layered in
cupcake form with a gratin crust

Ahi Tuna Tartar Cone
seared ahi tuna tartar served in
a baked petite sesame wonton cone

Grilled Polenta Sandwich
filled with smoky cheese
and sun-dried tomatoes

Shrimp Corn Pancake Parcel
grilled shrimp wrapped in a corn pancake
with coral sauce

Beef Tenderloin Yorkshire Pudding
Yorkshire puddings topped with
ribbons of medium rare beef tenderloin
and horseradish cream

Main

Maple Horseradish Lacquered Salmon
sides of salmon glazed with maple horseradish lacquer
served with red bell pepper tartar

Cosmopolitan Salad
seven leaf greens, candied pecans, dried cranberries
and goat cheese tossed in
absolut red wine dressing served in a cosmo glass

Grilled Chicken Satay
tangerine peanut sauce

Indulge

Retro Fruit Bowl
perfect shapes of
cantaloupe, honeydew and watermelon

French Macarons

Velvet Cupcakes
pink, orange and yellow velvet cupcakes

Libation

Mad 'V' Martini

SCALLOPS ON SUGAR CANE WITH LEMON GRASS CURRY MARINADE
Makes 20 scallops

20 scallops, 10/20 size, cleaned
10 sugar cane sticks, cut in half and carved into skewers

Curry Marinade

½ teaspoon coriander powder
½ teaspoon cardamom powder
½ teaspoon cumin
½ cup white onion, minced
1 teaspoon minced garlic
1 tablespoon grated ginger
¾ teaspoon chili powder
½ teaspoon ground black pepper
½ teaspoon ground turmeric
⅓ cup plain yogurt
2 tablespoons lemon juice
½ teaspoon salt
2 tablespoons fresh lemon grass, minced

Mix all the ingredients in a bowl. Adjust seasoning if needed.

Mango Chutney Dressing

¾ cup mayonnaise
3 tablespoons balsamic vinegar
3 tablespoons curry paste
3 tablespoons mango chutney
1 cup + 2 tablespoons olive oil

In a food processor, purée the mayonnaise, balsamic vinegar, curry paste, and mango chutney. Add the olive oil slowly until the mixture emulsifies. Check the seasonings and adjust as needed.

Put the curry marinade in a bowl with one cup of the mango chutney dressing. Add the scallops and marinate for at least 1 hour. Meanwhile, cut and carve the sugar cane sticks into skewers so that you can easily slide the scallops onto them. Remove the scallops from the marinade and sear them over high heat for 1 minute on each side. Cover the scallops with the remaining dressing and skewer them onto the sugar cane sticks and cook in a 350 degree oven for 3 minutes for the scallop to finish cooking and then serve.

MAC AND CHEESE CUPCAKE
Makes 25 individual cupcakes

⅛ cup butter

⅛ cup flour

1⅛ cups milk

1 bay leaf

Salt and white pepper to taste

1 cup grated yellow cheddar cheese

¼ cup grated parmesan cheese

½ cup Fontina or Swiss cheese

½ pound spaghetti pasta, cooked until soft

2 cups toasted breadcrumbs

1 tablespoon shredded cheddar cheese

1½ teaspoons chopped parsley

1½ teaspoons melted butter

In a sauce pan, melt the butter then whisk in the flour to make a roux, cook over medium heat for a few minutes. Add the milk and bay leaf and whisk constantly on high heat until it comes to a boil and starts to thicken. Turn the heat down to low, whisking frequently, for 10 minutes. Season to taste with salt and white pepper. Fold in the cheese while the sauce is still hot. Add the hot cooked spaghetti and mix well, set aside to cool. Prepare a mini muffin pan by spraying with non-stick spray and coating with the toasted breadcrumbs, reserve one cup of the toasted breadcrumbs for the topping. Once cooled, scoop the spaghetti mixture into the prepared mini muffin pans. In a bowl, mix together the reserved cup of breadcrumbs with shredded cheese, chopped parsley and melted butter. Cover the cupcakes with this topping and bake in a 350 degree oven for 10 to 12 minutes until heated through and serve. These can be made in advance and reheated just prior to serving.

AHI TUNA TARTARE CONE

Makes 24 tuna cones

12 wonton skins, each one cut into two triangles

Oil for frying

3 egg whites to adhere sesame seeds to the cones

½ cup white and black sesame seeds

Ahi Tuna Filling

¼ pound Ahi tuna (order sushi tuna "center cut")

1 tablespoon red onion, finely minced

1 tablespoon red bell pepper, finely minced

1 tablespoon scallions, sliced thin

1 tablespoon cucumber, finely diced

1½ teaspoons grated ginger

Tuna Marinade

½ cup soy sauce

½ cup rice wine vinegar

½ cup sesame oil

2 tablespoons Chili Oil *(see recipe index)*

Mix all of the ingredients for the marinade and set aside.

Prepare the tuna by trimming the skin and bloodline and cut it in half lengthwise. Marinate the tuna in 1 cup of the Tuna Marinade in a bowl for 1 hour, reserving the remaining marinade for later use. Remove the tuna from the marinade and sear in a hot pan or griddle for 1 minute on each side, set aside to cool. With a clean knife and cutting board, finely dice the tuna, then place in a bowl. Cut the vegetables into a very small dice and mix in with the tuna. Place the seared tuna and vegetables in the reserved marinade and let sit for 1 hour.

Meanwhile, make the cones. Fold the cut wonton skins into a cone shape and slide onto a piping tip to hold the shape. Place a little water on the wonton skin to stick the edges together. Brush the outside of the cone with a little egg white and sprinkle white and black sesame seeds on it. Place the cones in a fryer or a sauté pan with oil over very low heat and let brown evenly by rotating the cone around for about 5 to 7 minutes. Halfway through cooking, pull the cone out and remove the piping tip and place back into the fryer or pan until they become nice and crispy with a golden brown color. Place on a paper towel to dry.

To assemble, place the tuna mixture into the wonton cones and serve.

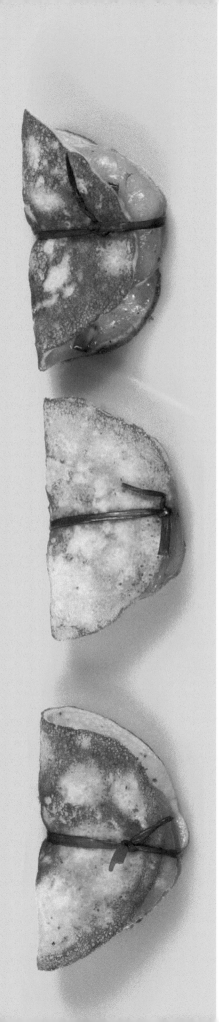

SHRIMP CORN PANCAKE PARCELS
Makes 25 pancakes

Pancakes

¼ cup corn

1 tablespoon butter plus butter for cooking the pancakes

¼ cup all-purpose flour

¼ cup corn meal

¼ cup milk

¾ cup water

2 large eggs

¼ teaspoon salt

Pinch of black pepper

Pinch of cayenne pepper

Sauté the corn on medium high heat for 5 to 7 minutes in the butter and set aside to cool. Place all of the ingredients into a food processor and blend together until the corn is mostly puréed. Always make the batter the day before and refrigerate overnight. Heat a non-stick griddle and melt a little butter in it. Using a ¼ ounce ladle, make a 2¼-inch pancake on the griddle and cook on both sides, making sure it is golden brown on each side. Set aside to cool. When cooled, layer the pancakes between sheets of parchment paper and wrap them in plastic wrap so that they are airtight. Keep at room temperature until it is time to assemble.

Coral Sauce

Makes 1 cup

¾ cup of mayonnaise

3 tablespoons American chili sauce

1 tablespoon roasted garlic purée

Salt and pepper to taste

Mix all the ingredients together and set aside.

Shrimp

25 peeled shrimp, size 21/25, deveined

1 gallon water

1 lemon

1 carrot, chopped

1 celery stalk, chopped

½ white onion, chopped

2 whole garlic cloves, chopped

2 bay leaves

10 black peppercorns

½ cup white wine

1 tablespoon garlic, minced

Salt and pepper to taste

2 tablespoons olive oil

25 long chives, blanched quickly in boiling water and then chilled in ice water.

Put water, carrots, celery, onions, whole garlic, bay leaves, peppercorns and white wine in a stock pot. Bring to a boil then lower the heat and simmer for 10 minutes before adding the peeled shrimp. Cook shrimp for 1 minute or until almost cooked and take the shrimp out of the liquid to cool. When cooled, mix the shrimp with ¼ cup of the Coral Sauce, 1 tablespoon minced garlic, olive oil and salt and pepper to taste. Sauté rapidly over high heat in a pan with olive oil for 3 minutes, in small batches, cooking fast so that the shrimp are seared for color but not overcooked. Remove from the heat and chill in the refrigerator until ready to assemble.

To assemble

Spread a ½ teaspoon of Coral Sauce on a pancake. Place 1 shrimp on each pancake and fold it over and tie with the blanched chive. You may need to cut a little off of the shrimp so that it fits nicely on the pancake.

GRILLED POLENTA SANDWICH WITH SMOKY CHEESE AND SUN-DRIED TOMATO

Makes 35 1-inch square sandwiches

2½ cups polenta (yellow cornmeal)

10 cups chicken broth

Pepper to taste (no salt)

½ cup chopped sun-dried tomato

2 cups grated parmesan cheese

2 tablespoons olive oil

1 cup Sun-Dried Tomato Aioli *(recipe to follow)*

70 slices smoked gouda cheese (cut to 1-inch squares)

Combine the polenta and broth in a saucepan. Cook over high heat, stirring constantly, until mixture comes to a boil (wearing oven mitts). Continue to cook over high heat, stirring constantly with a wooden spoon, for 20 to 30 minutes until creamy. Season with pepper, then add the chopped sun-dried tomato and parmesan cheese, stirring a little more to melt the cheese. Pour onto a 11x17-inch cookie sheet sprayed with non-stick spray. Cover with plastic wrap and chill overnight. Cut into 1-inch squares and then sear the squares on a hot griddle or pan with a little olive oil for 1 minute on each side. To assemble the sandwiches, place a dollop of Sun-Dried Tomato Aioli on a polenta square and then top with a 1-inch square slice of smoked gouda cheese, then another slice of polenta on top of that and a final slice of cheese on top of that. Warm the polenta sandwich under the broiler to crisp and brown the cheese and serve.

Sun-Dried Tomato Aioli

Makes 1 cup

¾ cup mayonnaise

1 tablespoon sun-dried tomato paste

2 tablespoons tomato paste

1 tablespoon roasted garlic

1 tablespoon lemon juice

Salt and pepper to taste

Place all ingredients in a food processor and blend until smooth. Check the seasonings and adjust as needed.

BEEF TENDERLOIN YORKSHIRE PUDDING WITH HORSERADISH CREAM
Makes 24 servings

2 pounds beef tenderloin

1 tablespoon olive oil

Salt and pepper to taste

24 Yorkshire Puddings *(recipe to follow)*

1½ cups Horseradish Cream
(recipe to follow)

5 chives for garnish

Clean the beef tenderloin of any fat and rub with the olive oil, salt and pepper. Tie the beef tenderloin in cooking string so that it holds the meat together. Sear on a hot griddle and then cook in the oven at 350 degrees for 20 to 30 minutes or until it reaches an internal temperature of 120 degrees. Take it out of the oven and let it rest for 15 to 30 minutes. When rested, slice all the beef on a meat slicer into paper thin slices. Set aside until ready to assemble.

To assemble, take a warm Yorkshire Pudding and pipe a dollop of Horseradish Cream into the bottom of the pudding. Then take some slices of beef, rolling them up and place inside the Yorkshire Pudding to just fill it to the top. Then place another dollop of Horseradish Cream on the top and garnish with some chopped chives.

Yorkshire Pudding
Makes 24 mini puddings (2 cups batter)

¾ cup flour

½ teaspoon salt

2 eggs

1 cup milk

2 cups vegetable oil

Make batter day before and refrigerate overnight. Blend the flour, salt, eggs and milk in a food processor for approximately two minutes until smooth, place in an airtight container and refrigerate overnight. Heat the mini muffin tins in the oven at 400 degrees for 20 minutes until they are very hot. Add ¼-inch of vegetable oil to each tin. Place the muffin pans back in the oven with the oil. Bake for another 20 minutes. Very carefully pull the muffin pans out of the oven and place 1 tablespoon of batter in each tin. Very carefully place it back into the oven and bake until the puddings are puffy brown and crisp, 10 to 15 minutes.

Horseradish Cream
Makes 1½ cups

¾ cup sour cream

1 teaspoon Dijon mustard

½ cup heavy cream, whipped

1 tablespoon red onion, minced

1 tablespoon parsley, minced

2 tablespoons grated horseradish

Salt and white pepper to taste

Whisk the sour cream and Dijon mustard together in a bowl. Fold in whipped cream, then fold in the minced red onions, parsley, horseradish, salt and pepper. Set aside.

MAPLE HORSERADISH LACQUERED SALMON
Makes 2 sides of salmon

2 sides of salmon, approximately 4 pounds, cleaned and skinned

1¼ cups pure maple syrup

¼ cup fresh lemon juice

2 tablespoons soy sauce

1 tablespoon horseradish (you can omit this if you like)

Red Bell Pepper Tartar *(recipe to follow)*

Simmer the maple syrup, lemon juice and soy sauce in a saucepan over medium heat until reduced by half. Add in the horseradish and let the sauce cool down to room temperature. Put the sauce away in a plastic container so that when you use it, you can put it in the microwave to warm it enough to make it pourable.*

Place the sides of salmon on a sheet pan sprayed with non-stick spray. Pour a half cup of very hot maple glaze on each side of the salmon. Don't try to spread it out, just put the tray in a 375 degree oven for 4 minutes. After the initial 4 minutes, pull out the tray and brush more glaze on top of the salmon every 2 minutes. It is very important to do this EVERY 2 MINUTES. After about 10 minutes, check to see if the salmon is almost done. Do not glaze again, cook for a few more minutes to set the glaze. Serve with Pink Peppercorn Sauce on the side.
Maple glaze can be kept for about 2 weeks.

Red Bell Pepper Tartar Sauce
Makes 2 cups

¼ cup roasted red bell pepper, diced

¼ cup dill pickle relish

¼ cup shallots, minced

⅓ cup sour cream

¼ cup parsley, chopped

2 tablespoons capers

½ teaspoon garlic, minced

¾ cup mayonnaise

Salt and white pepper to taste

Put all the ingredients in a food processor and mix lightly. You may leave it a little chunky if you desire. This can be made a few days ahead of the party.

GRILLED CHICKEN SATAY

Makes 25 chicken skewers

5 8-ounce chicken breasts cut into 10 thin slices each

25 6-inch wooden skewers

3 cups Tangerine Peanut Sauce *(recipe to follow)*

½ cup Vegetable Marinade *(see recipe index)*

Cut the chicken into thin slices lengthwise and weave two pieces on each skewer. Make the Peanut Sauce and marinate the chicken skewers in 1 cup sauce and ½ cup Vegetable Marinade for a few hours or overnight. Remove skewers from the refrigerator and discard any remaining marinade.

Cook the chicken by searing both sides of the skewer on a hot griddle for 1 minute on each side. Then coat again with the remaining Peanut Sauce and place the chicken skewers in a 350 degree oven for 7 to 10 minutes and serve.

Tangerine Peanut Sauce
Makes 3 cups

1 tablespoon vegetable oil

¾ cup shallots, minced

1 tablespoon fresh ginger, grated

1 tablespoon garlic, minced

½ serrano chili, chopped

1 teaspoon cumin

1 teaspoon ground coriander

1 teaspoon paprika

½ teaspoon black pepper

½ teaspoon salt

½ teaspoon cayenne pepper

1½ cups water

½ cup soy sauce

¾ cup peanut butter

½ cup brown sugar

¼ cup lemon juice

½ cup canned mandarin oranges, drained and puréed

¼ cup chopped cilantro

Heat the oil in a saucepan and add the shallots, ginger, garlic and serrano chili. Sauté for a few minutes until lightly brown. Add the spices and sauté a little more until the spice aromas are released, about 2 minutes. Add the water and soy sauce and mix together. Add the peanut butter and brown sugar and stir until dissolved. Then add the lemon juice and the mandarin orange purée and bring to a boil. Boil for about 1 minute, reduce the heat and simmer for 8 to 10 minutes until the sauce is a little thick. Let the sauce cool and add the cilantro.

COSMOPOLITAN SALAD
Makes 10 servings

1 pound seven leaf lettuce mix

2 cups Absolut Honey Red Wine Dressing *(recipe to follow)*

2 cups Candied Pecans *(recipe to follow)*

5 ounces goat cheese, crumbled

Toss everything together in a bowl and serve in a cosmopolitan glass with a fork.

Absolut Honey Red Wine Dressing
Makes 2 cups

⅓ cup red wine vinegar

¼ cup honey

¾ cup mayonnaise

1 tablespoon garlic, minced

1 teaspoon ground black pepper

⅓ cup olive oil

2 tablespoons Absolut vodka (optional)

In a food processor, blend the vinegar, honey, mayonnaise, garlic, salt and pepper.

Add the olive oil slowly until the dressing is smooth. Whisk in the vodka. Check seasonings and adjust as needed.

Spicy Candied Caramelized Pecans
Makes 2 cups

2 cups pecan halves

½ teaspoon black pepper

1½ teaspoons salt

⅛ teaspoon cayenne pepper

½ cup powdered sugar

4 cups canola salad oil (do not use liquid shortening)

Put the pecans in boiling water for one minute then drain. In a medium bowl, mix the pecans, pepper, salt, cayenne pepper and sugar. Heat the canola oil in a medium pot being careful to watch it so it does not get too hot and bubble over. Put the nuts in a deep fry basket and lower them into oil slowly. Fry until browned and the oil stops bubbling. Drain the nuts and spread on a sheet pan sprayed with non-stick spray for a few minutes. Separate the nuts with gloved hands or use tongs. Don't let the nuts stick together. When cool, let the nuts drain on paper towels until completely cool but, do not leave at room temperature too long or they will get soft. Store the nuts in an airtight container.

FRENCH MACARONS
Makes 28 cookies

⅓ cup unbleached almond flour

1 cup of confectioners sugar

½ vanilla bean

2 large egg whites

1 tablespoon granulated sugar

⅛ teaspoon food dye, your choice of color

5 tablespoons fruit jam (or you can use whatever filling that matches your color scheme)

Place the almond flour and the confectioners sugar in a food processor and blend until combined. Scrape the vanilla bean seeds from the pod and put into the food processor and pulse to combine. Transfer the mixture to a medium bowl. Fit a kitchen mixer with the whisk attachment and whisk the egg whites on medium speed until soft peaks form. With the mixer running, add half of the granulated sugar. Increase the speed to high and sprinkle in the remaining sugar. Continue to whisk until stiff peaks form. Place the whites on top of the almond flour mixture and fold them in, then add the food dye and fold to combine.

Line two baking sheets with parchment paper. Transfer the batter to a pastry bag fitted with a half inch tip and pipe 56 cookies onto each sheet. With one hand, hold the tip of the pastry bag perpendicular to and a ¼-inch above the baking sheet and apply even pressure to the end of the pastry bag with your other hand while slowly pulling the bag up from the baking sheet in order to pipe a one inch round macaron, move the bag in a circular motion as you pull it away to release the bag from the macaron. Continue piping the macarons, leaving 1 inch between them. Let the macarons sit at room temperature for 15 minutes to air-dry and form a light crust. Position the oven racks in the lower and upper thirds of the oven and pre-heat the oven to 325 degrees. Bake the macarons for 13 to 15 minutes, rotating the pan once halfway through baking. The macarons will be firm on the outside but the center should remain slightly soft.

To assemble the cookies, take one cookie and pipe the jam in the middle and then take another cookie and press the two cookies together gently to form a sandwich.

RETRO FRUIT BOWL
Makes about 5 quarts

1 cantaloupe, cut into circles

1 pineapple, cut into triangles

½ seedless watermelon, cut into squares

Peel the cantaloupe, scoop the middle out and scoop out with a melon baller. Peel the pineapple, cut out the center core, and cut into small wedges. Peel the watermelon and cut into medium size squares. In a bowl, toss the three fruits together and then place in individual serving dishes.

PINK, ORANGE OR YELLOW VELVET CUPCAKES

Makes 15 large cupcakes

½ cup butter

1½ cups sugar

2 eggs

1 teaspoon vanilla

2 tablespoons cocoa

2 tablespoons pink, orange or yellow food coloring

1 teaspoon salt

2½ cups all-purpose flour, sifted

1 cup buttermilk

1 teaspoon baking soda

1 tablespoon white vinegar

One small jar nonpareils *(available at specialty stores)*

Cream the butter and the sugar in a kitchen mixer with the paddle attachment. Add the eggs one at a time, beating well after each egg. Add the vanilla and mix in.

Make a paste of the cocoa and food coloring and add to the creamed mixture. Sift together the salt and flour and add it to the mixture alternating it with the buttermilk, beating well after each addition. Sprinkle the baking soda over the vinegar and pour over the batter and fold it in until thoroughly mixed.

Place the cupcake liners into the muffin pans and scoop the cupcake mixture into the cup cake holders. Bake in a 350 degree oven for about 12 minutes.

Frosting

Makes 3 cups

2 ounces butter, softened

8 ounces cream cheese

1 pound powdered sugar, sifted

Pinch of salt

½ teaspoon vanilla

Beat the butter with the paddle attachment in a kitchen mixer first if it is not already soft. Add the cream cheese to the butter and beat until mixed well. Add the sifted powdered sugar, salt and vanilla and mix until light and fluffy.

To assemble the cupcakes, take the cooled cupcake and pipe the frosting into a spiral on top. Sprinkle with nonpareils and serve.

THE MAD "V" MARTINI

2 ounces vodka

2 ounces white cranberry juice

½ ounce ginger elixir
(brand name Elixir G)

½ ounce pomegranate juice

Vanilla sugar for the rim

Rim your martini glass with vanilla sugar (see note). Fill a martini shaker with ice and pour in vodka, white cranberry juice, ginger elixir and pomegranate juice. Shake well and pour into your chilled martini glass and enjoy!

A note on vanilla sugar: Keep it on hand, it has lots of great uses. Cut a whole vanilla bean lengthwise and add to an airtight quart of white sugar. Keep it sealed for at least a few days before you enjoy it.

Invitations: Great ideas for great beginnings

Your invitation sets the tone of your party. It tells your invited guest why he or she will not want to miss THIS party. Because it is such an important component of a successful party, take time to personalize your invitation and give it your signature look. There are so many wonderful invitation companies that can guide you through the process, the wording and the etiquette of invitations.

There is a trend today towards people putting a very personal touch to their parties and it starts with the invitation. If your event is more informal, there are many on-line options through which you can create e-mail invitations. You can also consider making your own. This is especially easy if you are computer savvy.

To make your invitation stand out, focus on color, font and graphics. It helps to create a name or theme for your event and carry this through to the invitation and it's OK to stray from the norm. For instance, if it's a birthday party, consider sending an invitation that has a packet of seeds hot-glued to the inside and call your party "One to Grow On." Guests will love the fact that they can use the seeds and, as an added bonus, every time they see the flowers that grow, they'll think of you! I have also seen more extravagant invitations that are "green," such as living tree seedlings delivered with an invitation printed on recycled paper. Whatever you choose, the best rule of thumb is to make sure it fits the style of your party and your own personality.

If you want to be successful in getting attendance, try to include a hand-written note. It is so rare in these days of electronic communications to receive something hand written personally – I guarantee an RSVP.

WINE AND DINE
Picnic chic

Without a doubt my favorite beverage is wine! And my favorite party of all time is one that brings friends together over good wine, food and conversation. The dining table is my personal United Nations, bringing people together from all walks of life. Politicians talk about forging relationships "across the aisle," I say let's forge relationship "across the dining table!" It's easier and it always comes with a better menu! When bringing an eclectic group together, simplicity is the answer. That way you can concentrate on the people and not worry about the menu.

It was with this in mind that I planned an end-of-summer gathering for Kathy and David who wanted to host a party for some friends whom they thought would make a magical combination of people. Usually, Kathy and David prefer formal dining seating when they entertain but, because of the nature of the event, the summer temperature and the fact that their garden is an oasis in the city, I suggested a picnic instead. Being game for anything, their response was "Why not?"

Invitations were made by telephone in keeping with the casual nature. To add a sense of occasion, we named the event "Wine and Dine Picnic Chic!" When guests were told the theme, they instantly got it. Blankets and pillows were tossed artfully on the lawn and hampers were filled with bottles of wine and set among them. Benches, low wood tables and their own existing glass table and garden chairs were all used. We presented a buffet filled with food at room temperature so that no one was a slave in the kitchen during the party (beforehand was a different matter!) Once everyone was there and the food was out, all Kathy and David had to do was enjoy the evening and their guests.

We served a variety of Californian wines and added a sense of fun by providing guests with a rhubarb stick dipped in sugar and placed in the sparkling wine. The informality of the setting, the no-fuss menu and the beautiful summer night ensured that not only the wine, but the conversation, sparkled and bubbled along, creating that magical meeting across the table.

Menu

Main
Rack of Lamb with Chili Rub
roasted rack of lamb with five spice rub

Cranberry Quinoa
with dried cranberries, red onions, tomatoes,
cucumbers, mint, cilantro and honey lime dressing
served in individual "to go" boxes

Salmon with Fresh Lime Scallion Crust
pan roasted pacific salmon with lime zest
and chopped scallion crust

Buttermilk Fried Chicken
chicken dipped in buttermilk batter

Lavosh Beef Tenderloin Wrap
grilled ribbons of beef tenderloin wrapped in lavosh
with mushrooms, caramelized red onion, crumbled
stilton and watercress tossed in a horseradish mustard
vinaigrette dressing

Edamame Crostini
mashed edamame served on
grilled crostini toasts

Indulge
Cheesecake Brownies
chocolate brownie
with a swirl of New York cheesecake

Peanut Brittle
salted peanut brittle bark

Libation
Rhubarb Sparkling Wine Cocktail
chilled sparkling wine garnished
with fresh rhubarb wands
frosted with sugar

RACK OF LAMB WITH CHILI RUB

Makes 10 servings allowing 4 lamb chops per person

5 racks of lamb, approximately 7 to 8 chops per rack

Five Spice Rub
Makes 1½ cups

2 tablespoons salt

¾ cup paprika

3½ tablespoons ground cumin

1½ tablespoons ground ginger

1¼ teaspoons cayenne pepper

1½ tablespoons garlic, minced

1 cup olive oil

A selection of roasted chilies
(jalapeño, habanera, Serrano, Poblano, Anaheim etc.)

1 cup Vegetable Marinade *(see recipe index)*

Mix the five spices together with the garlic and olive oil in a bowl and set aside. Then take the racks of lamb and rub the five spice mixture over the rack being careful not to get it on the bones.

Sear the rack of lamb on a hot griddle for 3 minutes on each side until browned. Place onto a baking sheet and roast in a 375 degree oven for 20 to 25 minutes. Take the lamb racks out and let them rest for 10 minutes. Slice into chops, put on a platter.

Meanwhile, take the selection of chilies and toss them in 1 cup of the Vegetable Marinade. Grill the chilies on the griddle until they have nice grill marks on them and remove. Serve the chilies on the platter next to the lamb chops.

CRANBERRY QUINOA SALAD

Makes 12 cups or 22 small "to go" boxes

1 pound quinoa

3 cups chicken broth

2 cups salted water

¾ cup tomatoes, medium diced

¾ cup cucumber, medium diced

½ cup red onion, medium diced

½ cup dried cranberries

2 tablespoons cilantro leaves

2 tablespoons mint leaves

Honey Red Wine Dressing
(recipe to follow)

22 small "to go" boxes with a fork
(these are available at packaging or gift wrap stores or www.papermart.com)

Put the water and chicken broth in a pot and poach the quinoa gently until al dente, approximately 15 minutes. Strain out the liquid and chill the quinoa. Put the remaining ingredients in a large bowl and toss with the chilled quinoa. Drizzle your desired amount of dressing over the quinoa salad and toss until mixed well and serve.

Honey Red Wine Dressing:

1 tablespoon Dijon mustard

1 tablespoon honey

2 tablespoons lime juice

1 teaspoon garlic, minced

1 cup olive oil

In a food processor, make the dressing by combining all the ingredients except the olive oil. Add the olive oil slowly to the food processor until the dressing emulsifies.

BUTTERMILK FRIED CHICKEN
Makes 16 pieces

4 8-ounce chicken breasts cut into 2-ounce strips

4 cups buttermilk

1 tablespoon Tabasco

4 cups all-purpose flour

1 teaspoon cayenne pepper

1 tablespoon salt

1 tablespoon pepper

Soak the chicken strips in 2 cups of buttermilk, Tabasco and a sprinkle of salt and pepper for a few hours or overnight in the refrigerator.

In a bowl, mix the flour with cayenne pepper, salt and pepper and then spread out on a sheet pan. Take one piece of chicken at a time and roll it in the seasoned flour. Then dip the chicken in a bowl with the remaining 2 cups of buttermilk, and roll it again in the seasoned flour. Place on a clean pan. Keep each piece of chicken separated because they will stick together if they touch.

Heat oil in a fryer or pot to 300 degrees (do not overheat the oil as the chicken will burn on the outside and not cook in the middle). Fry the chicken until golden brown and lay it on paper towels to drain. You can fry the chicken an hour or so before your guests arrive, but don't refrigerate or the crust will become soggy.

SALMON WITH FRESH LIME SCALLION CRUST
Makes 10 servings

1 8 to10-pound Salmon, boned and skinless, cut into 2 sides

4 limes, zested

2½ cups parsley, chopped

2 cups green onions, chopped

½ cup fresh breadcrumbs

1 cup grated parmesan cheese

2 tablespoons garlic, minced

½ cup butter, melted

Salt and pepper to taste

Mix all ingredients except the salmon together in a bowl, check the seasonings and adjust if needed.

Place sides of salmon on a sheet pan sprayed with non-stick spray. Sprinkle the crumb mixture thickly onto the salmon, covering the top of the filet. Bake in a 375 degree oven for approximately 20 minutes. You can serve the salmon whole on platters or cut it into individual portions and serve.

BEEF WATERCRESS STILTON WRAP WITH ONIONS AND MUSHROOMS

Makes 12 servings

3 pounds beef tenderloin

2 tablespoons olive oil

6 pieces Lavosh

3 cups Champagne Dressing *(recipe to follow)*

2¼ cups sautéed mushrooms

2 cups caramelized onions *(see recipe index)*

2 cups stilton cheese, crumbled

4 cups watercress

Salt and pepper to sprinkle

Trim the beef tenderloin of any excess fat and tie with string to keep it together. In a pan, heat oil and sear the beef until it is browned on all sides, about 3 minutes each side. Place in oven at 375 degrees and roast until it reaches 120 degrees internally, about 20 minutes. Remove from the oven, cool and then slice thinly.

Lay the lavosh on a flat surface and brush each one with 2 tablespoons of Champagne Dressing. Place 3 ounces of sliced beef evenly across the bread and sprinkle with 3 tablespoons of sautéed mushrooms, 2 tablespoons of caramelized onions and 2 tablespoons of stilton cheese crumbles. Toss a little salad dressing on the watercress and place on top of the cheese.

Fold the ends of lavosh and roll until all the food is completely enclosed, then cut of the excess lavosh ends. Roll the lavosh wrap in wax paper and seal. Cut the wraps in half on a diagonal to show the spiral filling.

Champagne Dressing

Makes 3½ cups

4 tablespoons Dijon mustard

¾ cup champagne vinegar

1 tablespoon garlic, minced

3 cups olive oil

Salt and pepper to taste

Blend everything in a food processor except the olive oil. Slowly add the olive oil to the food processor until the dressing emulsifies.

EDAMAME CROSTINI

Makes 24 crostini

1 French baguette, sliced into 24 slices

1 cup butter, garlic and olive oil mixture, lightly warmed *(see recipe index)*

Salt and white pepper to taste

1 cup shelled raw edamame

¼ cup smoked almonds

¼ cup fresh mint leaves, chopped, reserving 1 tablespoon for garnish

½ cup extra virgin olive oil

2 teaspoons garlic, minced

Sea salt and coarsely ground black pepper to taste

To prepare the toasts, sliced the baguette and dip one side of each slice into the butter garlic olive oil mixture. Place on a sheet pan and sprinkle with salt and white pepper. Toast in a 300 degree degree oven for 10 to 15 minutes until crisp. Remove from the oven and set aside.

Place edamame, smoked almonds, fresh mint, garlic, salt, pepper and olive oil in a blender. Pulse the mixture until it is chunky and not smooth. Serve with toasted crostini garnished with a little chiffonade of mint.

CHEESECAKE BROWNIES

Makes 35 brownies

Brownies

½ pound butter or margarine

3¼ ounces semi-sweet chocolate chips

1½ teaspoons triple sec liqueur

1½ teaspoons light corn syrup

1½ teaspoons vanilla extract

⅔ cup all-purpose flour

½ teaspoon baking soda

¼ teaspoon salt

2 eggs

⅓ cup sugar

3 ounces dark chocolate chips

Cream Cheese Filling

4 ounces cream cheese

¼ cup sugar

1 egg

½ teaspoon vanilla extract

½ teaspoon brandy

½ cup sour cream

In a double boiler, melt the butter and semi-sweet chocolate chips together, stirring until smooth. Add the triple sec, corn syrup and vanilla extract and mix. Set aside to cool.

In a bowl, sift together the flour, baking soda and salt. In a separate bowl, mix together the eggs and sugar and beat until light and creamy. Add the chocolate mixture and the flour mixture to the creamed sugar and eggs, one third of the mixture at a time. Repeat until all the chocolate and flour are added.

Add the remaining dark chocolate chips to the batter. Divide the batter into two batches. Place one batch on a cookie sheet sprayed lightly with non-stick spray.

Prepare the cream cheese filling. Using a kitchen mixer with the paddle attachment, beat the cream cheese and sugar together until smooth. In a separate bowl, whisk together the eggs, vanilla and brandy and add it to the cream cheese mixture and whisk until well blended. Gently add the sour cream, making sure that all the lumps have blended into the mixture.

Spoon the cream cheese mixture and the remaining brownie mixture on top of the brownie batter that is already on the sheet pan in alternating dollops and swirl together with a knife to create a marbling pattern. Bake in a 300 degree oven for approximately 45 minutes until firm but not browned. Remove from the oven and cool. Cut into the shapes of your choice and serve.

PEANUT BRITTLE

Makes 3 cups

6 ounces salted peanuts

1 cup sugar

2 teaspoons fresh lemon juice

2 tablespoons water

½ teaspoon baking soda

Preheat the oven to 350 degrees. Place the peanuts on a sheet pan and toast for 8 to 10 minutes until golden brown. While the nuts are toasting, create your glaze.

Combine the sugar, lemon juice and 1 tablespoon of water in a small saucepan and bring the mixture to a boil. Swirl the pan occasionally, until the mixture turns a medium gold in color. Remove the pan from the heat and stir in the warm toasted nuts. Add the baking soda, which will make a froth and turn the glaze creamy.

Pour this mixture onto a well buttered baking sheet, spread it out and let it cool completely. When this peanut brittle is cooled, remove it from the baking sheet with a metal spatula, and bang lightly with a hammer until the pieces are sized to your liking.

How much wine?

As a lover of wine myself, there can never be too much wine at a party. After all, if you have chosen a good wine, you will continue to enjoy it well after the event. The trick here is to not run out! If you follow this rule of thumb, you will never have to send someone down to the store to pick up more wine:

Each standard 750 ml bottle of wine contains six glasses of a respectable four ounce serving. At a party you should allow that every guest will have a beverage of some sort every hour during the party. For a three hour party, you will need to allow half a bottle of wine per guest. Also allow the same amount of water per guest. Every group is different, so you should adjust the quantity based on your guest list. Generally, this guesstimate works.

It's all in a name

You may have noticed, throughout the various chapters of this book, that all of our events have a name around which the theme and the menu revolves. I always encourage clients to name their gathering, even if it is as traditional as "The Wedding Celebration of John and Clair." You can spice this up by adding a tag line such as "At last!" or "The Magic of Love" to it on the invitations and programs. If it fits the circumstance, a tagline can add another element or layer to the event. In some cases, it can be the entire reason for the party such as with the Good Spell Night party, the Fuel party or The New 30 party in previous chapters.

The next time you plan a party, think about the reason for the party and see if you can come up with a fun name to add to your event.

LOVE & MARRIAGE
For always

In 2008, Good Gracious! was in the unique position to coordinate and cater many same-sex marriages in California. Our clients, Kevin and Dennis, were one couple who planned the wedding of which they had always dreamed. Their idea was "think Cary Grant goes to the Vanderbilts for the weekend."

Twenty-six years ago they fell in love and had a child, Chelsea, who is genetically linked to them both with the help of the family. It had always been their dream to be married and declare their love for each other and for Chelsea in front of their friends and family. When they approached us, it was only six weeks from their wedding day. They said they wanted something simple but, as with any other wedding, it took on a life of its own. It became a massive production as they explored new ways to express themselves during the event.

We found a wonderful location overlooking the Pacific Ocean that allowed us the space to create all the elements Kevin and Dennis desired. Guests arrived at the valet and entered the estate onto a patio with a water fountain overlooking the ocean. We served them Blanc de Noir champagne embellished with an edible Hibiscus flower. They grazed on gourmet fare displayed in library shelves while jazz music played in the background. From there, they entered the ceremony area featuring an aisle runner stamped with a crest that had been customized for Kevin and Dennis. The ceremony went off without a hitch and as the sun set on the ocean, they said their vows. It was the perfect moment.

Dinner transitioned into an exquisitely designed forties supper club in a tent. Tables were set on tiers and they all faced the ocean and the central white dance floor. Dancing was the theme of the evening and the couple danced their first dance to Michael Buble's version of "Save the Last Dance for Me." During the evening, Chelsea performed for her fathers, along with four of the "Dancing with the Stars" professionals, to an appreciative audience.

All the senses were sated that day as we served a beautiful menu while a performer played sultry lounge music on a white baby grand piano. All that was left to supply was love and that was in abundance during the entire wedding, and will no doubt be for years to come.

DENNIS

KEVIN

Menu

Preview
served from an hors d'oeuvres library
Oyster Shooters
baby oysters with vodka, horseradish,
cocktail sauce, tabasco, lemon and parsley

Shades of Green Crudités Box
small white boxes filled with shades of green
crudités, green goddess dipping sauce

Spanakopita
wilted spinach and feta mixture
wrapped in a golden phyllo pastry

Begin
Soup and Salad Dynamic Duo
caprese stack of burrata cheese, heirloom tomato,
basil and aged balsamic coupled with the perfect
sip of smokey tomato soup presented in a demitasse
cup and a grilled smoked cheese and
sun-dried tomato pesto panini

Main
The Love of Beef
Guinness braised, english cut beef short rib and beef
tenderloin medallions wild mushroom demi glaze
with mashed potatoes and a haricot vert bundle

Grilled Black Cod
fresh pacific black cod on a bed of white bean tomato
stew with spinach and a haricot vert bundle

Indulge
The Love of Cookies and Strawberries
hazelnut shortbread, florentine brownie, coconut
macaroon, sugar heart cookies, thumb print cookies
and stemmed chocolate dipped and plain strawberries
on parchment liners printed with inspirational words

Libations
Chilled Beverages
lavender lemonade, cucumber water and
watermelon water

Sparkling Wine
edible hibiscus bloom

OYSTER SHOOTERS

Makes 12 shooters

12 small oysters, we use Fanny Bay

¾ cup vodka, use a premium brand

2 tablespoons cocktail sauce

2 tablespoons Tabasco

1 tablespoon horseradish

1 tablespoon lemon juice

Shuck the oysters from the shell using a shucking knife. Place an oyster in a shot glass. Add a splash of the vodka of your choice followed by a dash of cocktail sauce, a couple of drops of Tabasco, a dash of horseradish and then a splash of lemon juice. Refrigerate until needed. You may need some practice to make sure you balance the flavors so it comes together to your liking.

SHADES OF GREEN CRUDITÉ

Makes 12 servings

12 green beans or haricot vert, blanched

12 snow peas, blanched

12 green bell pepper sticks

12 leaves of endive, 3 inches long

12 green zucchini sticks

12 asparagus spears, 3 inches long

Green Goddess dressing *(recipe to follow)*

12 small plastic white or black boxes
(available on-line, we use www.sweetflavorfl.com)

Blanch the snow peas and asparagus in boiling water. Clean the remaining vegetables and cut into the desired sizes. We place one of each of the above shades of green vegetables in a small box with about 1 tablespoon of dressing in the base.

Green Goddess Dressing
Makes 1¼ cups

3 anchovy filets

¾ cup mayonnaise

¼ cup sour cream

4 tablespoons chives

4 tablespoons flat leaf parsley

1 tablespoon tarragon leaves

2 tablespoons basil

1 tablespoon shallots

1 tablespoons white wine vinegar

¼ teaspoon kosher salt

Freshly ground black pepper to taste

Combine all ingredients except pepper in a blender or food processor. Purée together to make a smooth dressing and season to taste with pepper.

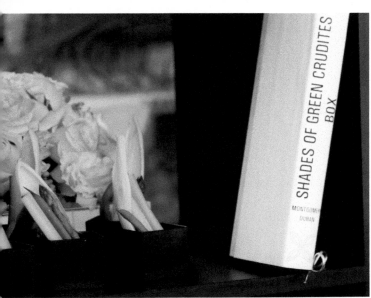

SPANAKOPITA

Makes 2 cups filling for 35 spanakopitas

¼ cup + 2 tablespoons butter, garlic, olive oil mixture
(see recipe index)

1 tablespoon garlic, minced

1 cup scallions, chopped (1 bunch)

4 ounces fresh spinach, chopped

1 tablespoon dill, chopped

2 eggs

Black pepper to taste

½ pound feta cheese, crumbled

20 14x18-inch phyllo sheets

1 tablespoon garlic, minced

Pour 2 tablespoons butter, garlic, olive oil mixture into a sauté pan, add the minced garlic, scallions, chopped spinach and dill and cook over low heat until wilted, about five minutes. Let it cool. Take the mixture and pulse in a food processor, adding the eggs, pepper and all of the feta cheese. Pulse together until chunky but not smooth. The flavor should be strong.

To assemble, take one sheet of phyllo dough and brush it with more butter, garlic, olive oil mixture. Repeat four times and stack the four sheets of phyllo on top of each other. Cut into rectangular shapes, approximately 2x8 inches. Place 2 teaspoons of the spinach mixture on each end of the phyllo rectangles and fold up into a triangle. Bake in a 375 degree oven for 15 minutes or until golden brown and serve.

CAPRESE STACK OF BURRATA CHEESE, HEIRLOOM TOMATOES AND BASIL WITH AGED BALSAMIC

Makes 10 servings

10 large fresh basil leaves, chiffonade

7 orange vine-ripened Heirloom tomatoes

1 pint burrata cheese

Sprinkle of black pepper and kosher salt

1 bottle aged balsamic glaze *(available at specialty stores)*

Basil olive oil *(recipe to follow)*

Slice the tomatoes to an even thickness. Place three slices of tomatoes on a dinner plate. Scoop 2 heaping teaspoons of burrata cheese on top of the tomatoes. Sprinkle with kosher salt and pepper. Drizzle with aged balsamic glaze and basil olive oil. Place a basil chiffonade on top.

Basil Oil
Makes 1 cup

1 cup extra virgin olive oil

1 small bunch of basil

Break up the basil by hand and rub it together to bring out the flavor. Warm the oil and basil together in a pot on low heat. After about 5 minutes, take the oil off the stove and cool. Store in an air tight container. The basil oil will keep for several weeks.

SMOKEY TOMATO SOUP

Makes 10 6-ounce servings

1 tablespoon olive oil

½ cup carrots, diced

¾ cup white onions, diced

½ cup celery, minced

1½ teaspoons garlic, minced

3 cups canned tomatoes with juice, diced

12 ounces tomato juice

2 cups chicken broth

1 cup beef broth

1 bay leaf

1 teaspoon rosemary, minced

2 tablespoons basil, minced

½ teaspoon thyme, minced

2 tablespoons tomato paste

¾ pounds smoked tomatoes *(recipe to follow)*

1 teaspoon granulated sugar

1 tablespoon lemon juice

1 pinch cayenne pepper

Salt and pepper to taste

GRILLED CHEESE SUN-DRIED TOMATO SANDWICH

Makes 5 sandwiches for 10 servings

1 loaf of Pullman white bread, thin sliced

¾ cup Sun-Dried Tomato Pesto *(recipe to follow)*

15 slices of smoked gouda cheese

½ pound butter

Place the bread slices on a flat surface and spread 1 tablespoon of Sun-Dried Tomato Pesto evenly on each slice of bread. Lay 2 slices of cheese on each slice of bread and then close the sandwiches. Spread a thin layer of butter on the outside of each slice of bread and grill the sandwiches in a panini maker. Cut the crusts off the sandwiches and cut into triangles. Allow 2 triangles per plate.

Sun-Dried Tomato Pesto

Makes 1 cup

4 ounces sun-dried tomatoes

4 tablespoons shredded parmesan cheese

1 teaspoon garlic, minced

4 tablespoons olive oil

Salt and pepper to taste

Soak the tomatoes in a bowl with boiling water for 1 hour until they are plump. Drain the tomatoes and peel off the skins. Place tomatoes, parmesan cheese and garlic in a food processor and purée. Add in the olive oil slowly to emulsify. Season with salt and pepper to taste.

Sauté the carrots, onions, celery and garlic with olive oil over medium heat in a soup pot. Cook until very tender, letting the vegetables sweat but not brown, about 20 minutes. Add the canned tomatoes, tomato juice, chicken broth, beef broth, bay leaf, rosemary, basil, thyme, tomato paste and smoked tomatoes and continue to simmer for about 1 hour. Add the sugar, lemon juice, salt, pepper and cayenne pepper and adjust the seasonings if needed. Let it cool slightly then puree in a blender, a little at a time until smooth.

Smoking Tomatoes

To smoke the tomatoes, I suggest using a stovetop smoker. It is available at camping supply stores and is a great low-cost cooking instrument. Place smoked chips in the smoker, put the rack into the smoker and lay sliced tomatoes on the rack. Season with sea salt, close the lid and smoke on the stove over medium to high heat for 4 to 5 minutes.

Another alternative would be to toss the tomatoes, cut in half, in liquid smoke and then roast them in the oven at 350 degrees for 10 minutes.

SHORT RIBS AND BEEF TENDERLOIN WITH MUSHROOM DEMI GLAZE

Makes 10 servings

Beef Tenderloin

1 whole beef tenderloin

Salt and pepper

Olive oil

Clean and trim any fat from the beef tenderloin. Cut the tenderloin in half lengthwise to create two longs strips. Tie each strip of tenderloin together with a string to hold its shape and brush it with olive oil. Sear the tenderloin on a hot pan or griddle for approximately 3 minutes on each side until browned. Place the tenderloins in a roasting pan and roast in a 375 degree oven until the internal temperature of the beef reaches 120 degrees, approximately 15 minutes. Remove from the oven, cut the string off and let it rest for about 5 minutes.

To serve, slice into medallions and lay 2 to 3 medallions on each plate.

Beef shortribs

10 English cut, meaty, bone-in short ribs

1 tablespoon coarse salt

Freshly ground black pepper

3 sprigs fresh rosemary, broken in half

2 bay leaves

¼ cup extra virgin olive oil

4 large yellow onions, sliced about ½-inch thick

2 cups carrots, chopped into ½-inch pieces

2 cups celery, chopped into ½-inch pieces

4 bottles of Guinness beer

6 cups beef stock, low sodium

2 cups water

Arrange the short ribs in a loose layer on a tray or non-reactive dish. Sprinkle with course salt and cover loosely with waxed paper or plastic wrap. Refrigerate for one day.

Heat the oven to 300 degrees. Pat the ribs dry with a paper towel, do not remove the salt, and sprinkle with pepper. Pour the oil into a 4 to 6 quart heavy braising pot. It should be wide enough to accommodate the short ribs. Place the ribs in the pot in a single layer, do not overcrowd. Sear the ribs on the stove over medium heat, browning until they are chestnut brown in color on all sides, about 4 minutes for each side. Transfer the seared ribs to a seperate large roasting pan and place them in one layer. Tuck the rosemary sprigs and bay leaves in between the ribs. Set aside.

Pour off and discard all but about 1 tablespoon of fat from the braising pot you used to sear the ribs. If there are any charred bits in the pot, wipe them out with a damp paper towel, being careful not to remove the precious caramelized drippings. Return the pot to the stove over medium-high heat, add the onions, carrots, and celery and season with salt and pepper. Sauté for 5 minutes, stirring a few times until the vegetables start to brown and soften. Add the beer and bring to a full boil, boil for 2 minutes. Pour in the stock and water, bring it to a boil again and reduce the heat to a simmer for 10 minutes. Pour the liquid mixture over the ribs. If necessary, add a bit more water to make sure that the ribs are fully submerged in liquid.

Cover the roasting pan with the ribs with a sheet of parchment paper, pressing the paper down so that it nearly touches the ribs and hangs over the edges of the pan by about an inch. Cover with foil and place in a 300 degree oven and braise at a gentle simmer. Turn the ribs with tongs, being careful not to tear the meat, every 40 to 45 minutes until fork tender, about 2½ hours. Check after the first 10 minutes to make sure that the liquid isn't simmering too aggressively. If it is, lower the oven temperature 10 or 15 degrees.

When the ribs are done, remove and set aside. Strain the vegetables from the pot and add the liquid back in. Tilt the pot to collect the juices in one end and skim off as much surface fat as you can with a large spoon. If the braising liquid exceeds a ½ cup, bring the liquid to a simmer over medium heat and cook for 10 minutes to reduce slightly.

To serve the ribs, brush them with the braising liquid to give the meat a nice color. Serve on a plate with the Beef Tenderloin and drizzle both with the Mushroom Demi Glaze Sauce *(recipe to follow)*, top with a Haricot Vert Bundle and serve with Mashed Potatoes *(see recipe index)*.

Mushroon Demi Glaze Sauce
Makes 1 quart

1 tablespoon butter

2 medium carrots, peeled and diced

1 yellow onion, peeled and diced

1 stalk celery, diced

1 medium shallot, minced

½ cup brandy

3 cups chicken broth

3 cups beef broth

3 bay leaves

½ bunch parsley stems

½ small bunch fresh thyme

3 cloves of garlic

1 teaspoon black peppercorns

½ cup dried porcini mushrooms (boil in some water to rehydrate)

½ cup veal glace de viande (available in specialty stores)

½ cup flour

½ cup soft butter

Melt the butter in a saucepan over medium heat, then add carrot, onion, celery and shallot and cook until tender and light brown, about 10 minutes. Add the brandy and reduce the sauce by half. If the flame catches to the brandy, you can wait while it burns out and then continue reducing.

Add the chicken broth, beef broth, herbs, garlic and porcini mushrooms. Bring to a boil, reduce heat and simmer for 1 to 2 hours over low heat. Strain the sauce, discarding vegetables, and put it back in the saucepan. Bring back to a boil, turn down to a simmer and add the glace de viande.

While this is simmering, mix together the butter and flour to create a roux and then whisk the roux into the sauce to thicken it. Cook over low heat for a couple minutes longer to eliminate the raw flour taste. Taste for seasoning and adjust if needed. You can serve the sauce right away or cool it to serve later.

GRILLED BLACK COD

Makes 10 servings

10 6-ounce portions black cod, skin
removed

2½ cups Vegetable Marinade
(see recipe index)

1 leek, frizzled

6 cups White Bean Stew
(recipe to follow)

2½ cups Beurre Blanc Sauce
(recipe to follow)

10 Haricot Vert Bundles
(see recipe index)

Marinate the cod in Vegetable Marinade for 24 hours. Remove from the marinade and sear the cod on the grill to get the criss cross lines on top. Then place the cod in a 350 degree oven for 7 to 10 minutes.

To frizzle the leek, cut the green leafy part off the leek and discard. Take the white stalk and cut off the bottom stem. Slice the white leek lengthwise in half. Cut the halves into three equal pieces each. Thinly slice each piece lengthwise to create small strips.

Heat a fryer or pan with oil at very low temperature, about 250 degrees, and fry the leeks until light golden brown with a little color, about 3 minutes. Remove from the oil and drain on a paper towel.

White Bean Stew
Makes 6 cups

1 tablespoon butter

½ carrot, cut in half inch dice

½ celery stalk, cut in half inch dice

3 shallots, cut in half inch dice

¼ cup Spanish sherry

12 ounces northern white beans, dried

4 cups of chicken broth

3 cups water

4 ounces diced tomatoes from the can, no juice, cut in half inch dice

4 ounces fresh spinach

Salt and pepper to taste

2 tablespoons butter

In a heavy duty stock pot on medium heat, sauté the butter, carrots, celery and shallots for 10 minutes. When the vegetables are a nice brown color, deglaze the pan with dry sherry. Rinse the white beans in water and add them to the vegetables. Add the chicken broth and water. Bring to a boil and reduce the heat and simmer for 45 minutes or until the beans are al dente, then add the tomatoes. The beans are always better cooked the day before you plan to serve them. To serve, sauté the fresh spinach in a little butter, salt and pepper until just wilted, about 3 minutes. Fold the spinach into the stew and serve.

Beurre Blanc Sauce
Makes 2½ cups

2 shallots, minced

1¼ cup white wine vinegar

1¼ cup white wine

¾ cup heavy cream

¾ pound cold butter, diced

Salt and white pepper to taste

4 tablespoons lemon juice

Place the shallots, white wine vinegar and white wine in a saucepan and bring to a boil and reduce by half. Add the cream and reduce the sauce to ¾ cup. Check this amount by pouring the sauce into a measuring cup. If needed, place the sauce back in the pan and reduce a little longer. To save time, you can make the reduction ahead of time and finish the sauce later when ready to serve.

Whisk in the butter, a little at a time or the sauce will break, over low heat until the acidic taste is removed from the sauce. Add the lemon juice, salt and white pepper to taste. This sauce must be served immediately or the sauce will break.

To serve, spoon the White Bean Stew in the bottom of a bowl and top with the Grilled Black Cod. Drizzle with Beurre Blanc Sauce and top with a small handful of frizzled leeks. Accent with a Haricot Vert Bundle and serve.

HAZELNUT SHORTBREAD COOKIES

Makes 25 small cookies, 2½-inches

7 ounces soft butter

¾ cup + 1 tablespoon powdered sugar, sifted

5 teaspoons cornstarch

2 cups cake flour, sifted

½ teaspoon baking powder

1 cup melted dark chocolate

½ cup toasted hazelnuts, chopped

Cream the butter in a kitchen mixer with the paddle attachment. Sift the powdered sugar, cornstarch, cake flour and baking powder together in a bowl and then add to the butter and mix well. Place the cookie dough in a piping bag with a plain tip. Pipe the dough into 2½-inch cookies on a sheet pan lined with parchment paper. Bake in a 325 degree oven for 10 to 12 minutes until a light golden brown. Remove from the oven and set aside on racks to cool.

When cooled, take one side of the cookie and dip it into the melted chocolate. Making sure you cover ¼ of the cookie with the chocolate. Then sprinkle the chocolate covered area of the cookies with chopped hazelnuts.

FLORENTINE BROWNIES

Makes 9x13-inch pan cut into 48 triangles

5 ounces butter

⅔ cup cocoa

2 eggs

1 cup granulated sugar

¾ cup sifted all-purpose flour

½ teaspoon vanilla

2½ ounces toasted hazelnuts, chopped

Melt the butter and cocoa together in a double boiler. Beat the eggs and sugar together in a kitchen mixer with the paddle attachment until thick and fluffy. Add the melted chocolate mixture to the egg and sugar mixture and scrape down the sides of the bowl and mix well. Add the flour, vanilla and chopped hazelnuts and mix well.

Spray the 9x13-inch pan with non-stick spray and line with parchment paper. Spread the batter evenly. Bake in a 325 degree oven for 15 to 18 minutes. When cool, cut the brownies into triangles.

COCONUT MACAROONS

Makes 30 macaroons

2½ cups shredded coconut

1 cup granulated sugar

½ cup all-purpose flour

½ teaspoon salt

2 eggs

½ teaspoon vanilla extract

Mix the dry ingredients together in a bowl. In a separate bowl, mix together the vanilla and eggs. Add this to the dry ingredients and mix well.

Scoop the mixture with a #70 scoop or rounded tablespoon, roll into a ball and place on a sheet pan sprayed with non-stick spray and covered with parchment paper. Bake in a 350 degree oven for approximately 12 to 15 minutes until nice and golden brown.

SUGAR COOKIES

Makes 30 heart-shaped cookies

½ cup butter

1 cup granulated sugar

2 beaten eggs

2½ cups all-purpose flour

2 teaspoons baking powder

2 tablespoons milk

½ teaspoon vanilla

½ teaspoon brandy

½ cup crystal sugar *(available in specialty stores)*

Cream the butter and sugar in a kitchen mixer with the paddle attachment until light and fluffy. Add the eggs slowly, with the mixer is still running, and scrape down the sides of the bowl after each one is added. Sift the flour and baking power in a bowl. Add half of the flour mixture and half of the milk, vanilla and brandy and then scrape down the bowl again. Add the rest of the flour and milk. Beat for few minutes. Take the dough out, cover in plastic wrap, flatten out and put in the refrigerator to chill for one hour.

On a lightly floured surface, roll the dough out to ¼ inch, and cut into any shape you want. Brush with a little milk and cover it with crystal sugar. Bake in the oven at 325 degrees for 10 minutes until golden brown.

PEANUT THUMBPRINT COOKIES

Makes 25 cookies

4 ounces butter

¼ cup brown sugar

½ cup peanut butter

1 egg

1 teaspoon vanilla extract

2 cups sifted all-purpose flour

1 cup peanuts, ground

Dark Chocolate Ganache *(recipe to follow)*

In a kitchen mixer with the paddle attachment, cream together butter and sugar until light and creamy. Add the peanut butter to the mixer and mix well to blend. Then add the egg and vanilla and mix well. Sift the flour and add a little at a time.

Scoop the dough with scoop size #100 or rounded teaspoons. Roll the dough into balls, and then roll the balls in the chopped peanuts to coat. Make a hole in the center of each ball with a wooden spoon handle or your thumb. Bake in the oven at 325 degrees for 12 minutes. When the cookies have cooled, pipe the Dark Chocolate Ganache into the hole in the center of each cookie.

Dark Chocolate Ganache
Makes 1½ cups

¾ cup heavy cream

2 tablespoons light corn syrup

7 ounces dark chocolate, chopped

Bring the cream and light corn syrup to a boil in a pot. Add the chocolate, remove from the heat and cover. Let it sit until all the chocolate is melted. Whisk together until smooth.

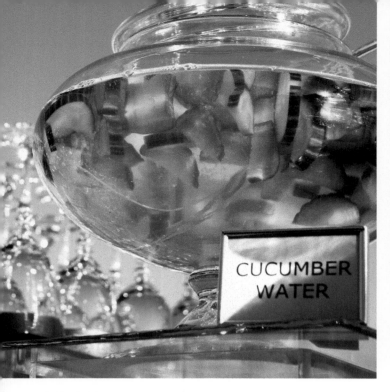

CHILLED BEVERAGES

Lavender Lemonade

8 cups lemonade

4 sprigs fresh flowering lavender

Make lemonade and place in a pitcher. Take the lavender sprigs, break up some of the pieces and put into the lemonade. Add in the remaining full sprigs and serve.

Cucumber Water

8 cups spring water

1 whole English cucumber, thinly sliced

Mix water and cucumber in a pitcher and chill for at least one hour.

Watermelon Water

6 cups spring water

2 cups fresh seedless watermelon, chopped

½ cup granulated sugar

Mix all the ingredients in a blender and puree. Place in a pitcher with ice and serve.

SPARKLING WINE WITH EDIBLE HIBISCUS BLOOM

1 bottle premium sparkling wine (we use schramsberg blanc de noir)

1 small jar Wild Hibiscus *(www.wildhibiscus.com)*

Arrange 6 champagne flutes on a tray and place one Wild Hibiscus flower in the bottom of each flute. Gently pour the champagne into the glasses and serve.

Discuss service with your caterer!

In this day and age, one probably thinks it is not necessary to ask about service styles as the caterer should know exactly what to do. To me it is very important to discuss service as you need to be sure that your expectations are met.

A traditional sit-down service would have waiters placing meals from the left and removing plates from the right. This works fine, but at Good Gracious! we have found that serving and removing from the right relieves guests from guessing which direction the waiter will come from next.

Here are some items to discuss with your caterer:

Should ladies be served first or should waiters simply start with a point person and continue around the table regardless of sex?
We like to choose a point person at the table and serve in a clockwise direction as it quickens service

Should water be filtered? Should it be served chilled or over ice?
I personally prefer water to be filtered and chilled as pouring water over ice creates condensation on the glass that drips on the tablecloth, leaving water stains. It ruins the lovely table top display.

Do you want lemon in the water?
I do not like serving lemon in the water as it creates another flavor to compete with the food.

As the host, do you want your table served first?
According to etiquette, the host is the first person to be served, allowing him or her to make sure the plate presentation is to their liking and that you are serving the food ordered.

Do you want plates removed as each guest finishes or clear the plates when the whole table is finished?
This is your preference, but in our experience most people like to wait until the whole table has finished eating. If you are on a timeline and have to hasten service, we suggest removing as each guest finishes. A signal to a wait-person that you have finished eating is placing your fork and knife together at the 6 o'clock position on your plate.

Do you want a bread and butter plate?
I am of the opinion that on many occasions, the table is full of beautiful specialty items and the bread and butter plate makes the table look and feel crowded. It also means that bread crumbs are inevitable as is smashed butter. My preference is to serve breadsticks or crostini with the first course. I promise you that during a fine meal, the bread will not be missed.

Why hire a planner
As many brides and grooms will tell you, there is so much to do for your wedding that it can all become overwhelming. Plus, it's not every day that you host a party of this caliber, size or of this importance.

Planners arrange events on a regular basis and, in addition to understanding logistics and timing, have their ears to the ground for the best resources, the latest looks and are the savviest advisors. Planners guide couples through the waters of wedding planning from beginning to end – from finding the perfect location to offering suggestions for the perfect honeymoon location. Finding the right planner who understands you, your personality and how you want to express your love to your friends and family will be your first important union.

RECIPE INDEX
Recipes referenced in Food, Fun, Love

SHORTCRUST PASTRY
Makes 20 cups mix

4 pounds all-purpose flour

2 pounds cold butter

Mix the flour and butter with an electric mixer, using the paddle attachment, on low speed until mixed thoroughly and is crumbly. This mixture can be stored for later use. To form the dough, take 4 cups of the short crust mix and knead with ½ cup water to form a dough. Once the dough is formed, roll it out to the desired thickness and cut.

VEGETABLE MARINADE or ALL PURPOSE MARINADE
Makes 1 gallon

4 cups white wine

1 cup red wine vinegar

¼ cup Dijon mustard

¼ cup garlic, minced

¼ cup paprika

¼ cup rosemary, minced

¼ cup thyme, minced

8 cups olive oil

Salt and pepper to taste

Place all the ingredients, except the olive oil, in a container. Whisking by hand, slowly add the olive oil, stirring to emulsify. Marinade can be stored in an air tight container in the refrigerator for several weeks.

BUTTER, GARLIC, OLIVE OIL MIXTURE
Makes 2 quarts

1 pound butter

¼ cup garlic, minced

8 cups extra virgin olive oil

Put all the ingredients into a heavy duty pot and bring to a boil. Remove from the heat and skim off the top. Set aside to cool. Place in an airtight container and store in the refrigerator until ready to use. This mixture will keep for about 4 weeks.

ROASTED GARLIC CLOVES

Makes 1 quart whole cloves

2½ pounds peeled garlic cloves

½ cup olive oil

Place garlic and oil in a metal baking pan, cover with foil and bake at 325 degrees for 1½ to 2 hours until very soft. Drain oil. Store cloves in an airtight container in the refrigerator until ready to use. Cloves can be stored for several weeks or frozen.

SIMPLE SYRUP

2 parts water

1 part granulated sugar

Put the water and sugar together in a sauce pan over low heat on the stove. When the sugar is dissolved, turn the heat up to high and bring to a boil. Remove from the heat and cool. The syrup is now ready to use. Syrup can be kept in the refrigerator for 5 days.

POACHING LIQUID

1 gallon water

1 carrot, chopped

1 celery stalk

½ white onion

2 whole garlic cloves

2 bay leaves

10 black peppercorns

½ cup white wine

1 lemon, cut in half

Place the water, carrot, celery, onion, whole garlic, bay leaves, peppercorn and white wine into a stock pot. Squeeze the lemon juice into the stockpot and then put the rest of the lemon in also. Bring to a boil and then reduce the heat and simmer for 10 minutes. At this point, the liquid is ready to poach your ingredients.

EGG WASH

1 egg

1 tablespoon milk

In a bowl, whisk together the egg and milk. Use this wash to brush onto pastry to adhere or create a shiny surface.

CARAMELIZED ONIONS

Makes 2 cups

2½ pounds sliced onions

½ cup granulated sugar

½ cup red wine vinegar

½ cup water

¼ pound butter

Salt and pepper to taste

Place all the ingredients in a heavy pot and cook, covered, over medium heat until the onions are very soft, about 3 hours, stirring occasionally. Then uncover, turn the heat up to medium high and continue cooking until the onions are soft and brown and no liquids remains. Stir constantly so the onions don't burn. Cool and puree lightly in a food processor. Store in an airtight container in the refrigerator until ready to use. Onions can be stored for several weeks.

CHIMICHURRI SAUCE

Makes 1½ cups

1 cup packed cilantro (1 bunch, don't cut)

1 cup packed parsley (1 bunch, don't cut)

2 tablespoons pickled ginger (with juice)

1 tablespoon garlic, minced

½ Serrano chili, roasted peeled and seeded

1 tablespoon yellow miso paste

¼ cup lemon juice

½ cup extra virgin olive oil

Salt and black pepper

Chop the parsley and cilantro in a food processor. Add the ginger, garlic, chili, miso paste and lemon juice. Puree until smooth. Add the olive oil to the food processor slowly to emulsify the mixture. Season with salt and pepper to taste. The flavor should be sharp and lemony. This can only be made the same day as it discolors by the next day.

HARICOT VERT BUNDLES

Makes 10 servings

120 haricot vert or tiny green beans

12 fresh chives, blanched

Salt to taste

Rinse the haricot vert and remove the stems. Place them in a pot of salted boiling water and boil for three minutes. Immediately remove the beans and place into an ice water bath to stop the cooking process. Drain the beans and pat dry. Blanch the chives in the same water for 30 seconds and then place then into the water bath. Drain and pat dry. Take one chive and place 12 beans in the center of the chive in a bundle, all facing the same direction. Wrap the chive around the bundle two times and tie in a tight knot. Just prior to serving, quickly drop the bundles into rapidly boiling water for three minutes to heat through. Remove, drain and serve.

MASHED POTATOES

Makes 10 servings

7 russet potatoes

½ cup heavy cream

¼ pound butter, softened

1 tablespoon roasted garlic puree

Salt and pepper to taste

Peel potatoes and cut into large chunks. Boil in salted water for 30 minutes or until soft. Drain and place potatoes back into the pot. Mash the potatoes, add cream, butter, garlic, salt and pepper to taste.

CHILI OIL

¼ cup vegetable oil

1 teaspoon sesame oli

2 teaspoons dried red pepper flakes

Heat oil over medium heat. Add red pepper flakes and remove from heat. Cool and strain, discarding the red pepper flakes. Chili oil can be stored at room temerature for several months.

LAYERED POTATOES

Makes 10 servings in a 9x9-inch baking pan

4 to 5 russet potatoes

1 tablespoon butter

1 tablespoon garlic, minced

1 tablespoon fresh sage, thinly sliced

2 cups heavy cream

Salt and pepper

1½ cups breadcrumbs mixture

Preheat oven to 350 degrees. In a heavy duty pot, heat the cream until hot, set aside. Prepare your baking pan by rubbing with butter and sprinkling with garlic. Peel the potatoes and place in a bowl of water to keep potatoes from browning. Place a ladle of hot cream into the baking pan to cover the bottom. Take 2 potatoes and slice very thinly on a mandolin or with a knife and layer into the pan. Cover lightly with cream and sprinkle with salt and pepper and sage. Repeat the process, without the sage, until done. Lightly press down on the potatoes to compact them and allow the cream to rise to the top. Add additional cream if needed. Cover with wax paper and foil. Bake at 350 degrees for 1½ hours until the potatoes are soft. Remove the paper and cover with the breadcrumb topping. Continue to bake uncovered for 10 to 15 minutes until golden brown. Cut into 10 servings.

BREAD CRUMBS MIXTURE

Makes 1½ cups

1½ cups fresh breadcrumbs

1 teaspoons garlic, minced

1½ tablespoons melted butter

Mix together all ingredients together in a bowl. Spread over the layered potatoes.

GLOSSARY
Commonly used terms

Al Dente
An Italian phrase meaning "to the tooth" used to describe pasta or other food that is cooked only until if offers a slight resistance when bitten into which is not soft or overdone.

Aji Amarillo paste
One of the staples in Peruvian cooking is the Aji Amarillo pepper. In English, this would be the yellow chili pepper, but they can be orange, yellow or green. Here we also use peppers such as Aji Limo, Rocoto, Charapa and so many more. An Aji yellow pepper roasted and pureed.

Bain Marie
The French term for a water bath. It consists of placing a container (pan, bowl, soufflé dish, etc) of food in a large shallow pan of warm water, which surrounds the food with gentle heat.

Blanch
To plunge food (usually vegetables and fruits) into boiling water briefly. Then into cold water to stop the cooking process.

Bloom
To moisten gelatin in a small amount of water before dissolving it in hot liquid.

Branston Pickle
A well known United Kingdom brand of savory food. They are most well known for their original Branston Pickle, a jarred pickled relish first made in 1922 in the Branston suburb of Burton upon Trent by Crosse & Blackwell. Branston Pickle is sweet and spicy with a chutney-like consistency, containing small chunks of vegetables in a thick brown sticky sauce. It is commonly served as part of a Ploughman's lunch, a once common menu item in British pubs. It is also frequently combined with cheddar cheese in sandwiches, and most sandwich shops in the UK offer "cheese and pickle" as an option.

Chiffonade
Literally translated this French phrase means "made of rags". Culinary, it refers to thin strips or shreds of vegetable (classically, sorrel and lettuce), either lightly sautéed or used raw to garnish soups, salads and other dishes.

Concassé
A mixture that is coarsely chopped or ground. The classic concasse is comprised of tomatoes that have been peeled, seeded and chopped.

Deglaze
After food (usually meat) has been sautéed and the food and the excess fat is removed from the pan, deglazing is done by heating a small amount of liquid in the pan and stirring to loosen browned bits of food on the bottom. The liquid used is most often wine or stock. The resultant mixture often becomes the base for a sauce to accompany the food cooked in the pan.

Double boiler

A double pan arrangement whereby two pots are formed to fit together, with one sitting partway inside the other. A single lid fits both pans. The lower pot is used to hold simmering water, which gently heats the mixture in the upper pot. Double boilers are used to warm or cook heat sensitive food such as custard, delicate sauces and chocolate. You can even make a double boiler by placing a metal bowl over a pot of simmering water.

Ficelle

French for "twine or string", a culinary term referring to a long, very thin loaf of French bread, about half the size of a baguette.

Flatbread

A generic term for bread that is thin and flat, leavened or not. Breads like Chaoati, Focaccia, Fougasse, Lavish, Naan, Pita and pizza are often referred to as flatbread.

Herbes de Provence

An assortment of dry herbs said to reflect those most commonly used in southern France. The blend can be found packed in tiny clay crocks in the spice section of large supermarkets. The mixture commonly contains basil, fennel seed, lavender, marjoram, rosemary, sage, summer savory and thyme. The blend can also be used to season dishes of meats, poultry and vegetables.

Julienne

Foods that have been cut into thin, matchstick strips. The food (such as a potato) is first cut into ⅛-inch thick slices. The slices are stacked, and then cut into ⅛-inch thick strips. The strips may then be cut into whatever length is desired. If the object is round, cut a thin slice from the bottom so it will sit firmly and not roll on the work surface.

Mâche

Also known as corn salad, field salad, field lettuce, lamb's lettuce. Native to Europe, mache is used in salads. The narrow, dark green leaves of this plant are tender and have a tangy, nutlike flavor. In addition to being used as a salad green, mache can also be stemmed and served as a vegetable. Though it's often found growing wild in American corn fields, it's considered a "gourmet" green and therefore expensive and hard to find.

Mandoline

A compact, hand operated machine with various adjustable blades for thin to thick slicing and for julienne and French-fry cutting. Mandolines have folding legs and come in both plastic and stainless steel frame models. They're used to cut firm vegetables and fruits (such as potatoes and apples) with uniformity and precision. On most machines, the food is held in a metal carriage on guides so that fingers aren't in danger. A less expensive option is the Japanese Mandoline which works the same as the French Mandoline.

Muscat wine

A rich, sweet dessert wine created from the Muscat grape. It's made from both the black and white varieties, so its color can range from golden to amber to pale amber red. Muscat's flavor typifies the characteristically musty flavor of the Muscat grape.

Panini maker

Panini means traditional, small Italian sandwich filled with meat, cheese, grilled vegetables, etc., and usually toasted. A toaster or press that sandwiches and presses down the sandwich as it toasts.

Riesling wine

Riesling is considered one of the world's great white wine grapes and produces some of the very best white wines. It is native of Germany, where it is believed to have been cultivated for at least 500 and possibly as long as 2,000 years. Riesling wines are delicate but complex, and characterized by a spicy, fruit flavor, flower - scented bouquet and long finish. Riesling is vinified in a variety of style ranging from dry to very sweet.

Roux

A mixture of flour and fat that after being slowly cooked over low heat, is used to thicken mixtures such as soups and sauces. There are three classic roux - white, blond and brown. The color and the flavor is determined by the length of the time the mixture is cooked. Both white roux and blonde roux are made with butter. The former is cooked just until it begins to turn beige and the latter until pale gold. Both are used to thicken cream and white sauces and light soups, the full flavored brown roux can be made with butter, drippings, or pork or beef fat. It's cooked to a deep golden brown and used for rich, dark soups and sauces.

Sauté

To cook food quickly in a small amount of oil or other fat in a skillet or sauce pan or sauté pan over direct heat.

Scoops

Ice cream scoops come in a variety of sizes such as 24, 40, 50, and 70. You can find these in specialty kitchen supply stores.

Silpat mat

The brand name of an FDA-approved nonstick baking and countertop sheet produced by several manufacturers. It's made of silicone with reinforced glass weave. It does not require greasing and provides an even heat transfer. Silpat is effective at temperatures ranging from 40°F to 480°F. Silpat mats can be found at gourmet shops and many department store kitchenware sections.

Slurry

A thin paste of water and starch (flour, cornstarch or arrowroot), which is added to hot preparations (such as soups, stews and sauces) as a thickener. After the slurry has been added, the mixture is typically stirred and cooked for a few minutes in order to thicken and loose any raw taste.

Unsalted Butter

Unsalted butter is used in all of our recipes. We add in salt, to taste, to each recipe as needed. If you use salted butter then you can taste your recipe and adjust with additional salt as needed.

ACKNOWLEDGEMENTS

Photography by Will Henshall of Henshall Photography

All events were produced and catered by
Good Gracious! Events

GOOD SPELL NIGHT
Classic Party Rentals, www.classicpartyrentals.com

Washington Place Florals, www.washingtonplaceflorals.com

FUEL
Liese Gardner, host

Town and Country Event Rentals,
www.townandcountryeventrentals.com

LADIES WHO DO TEA
Annette Groen, host

The Hidden Garden Floral Designs,
www.hiddengardenflowers.com

CALIFORNIA BAJA POOLSIDE
Janie and Christian VanFleet, hosts

Classic Party Rentals, www.classicpartyrentals.com

Rrivre Works Event Design and Prop Rentals,
www.rrivreworks.com

Washington Place Florals, www.washingtonplaceflorals.com

THE NEW 30
Dan Smith and Andrew Munoz, hosts

Classic Party Rentals, www.classicpartyrentals.com

Washington Place Florals, www.washingtonplaceflorals.com

Wildflower Linen, www.wildflowerlinens.com

James Hickey, www.henshallphotography.com

SUNDAY KIND OF LOVE
Bruce and Janette Carpenter, hosts

Classic Party Rentals, www.classicpartyrentals.com

Washington Place Florals, www.washingtonplaceflorals.com

Wildflower Linen, www.wildflowerlinens.com

CITY WAREHOUSE
Rrivre Davies, host

Rrivre Works Event Design and Prop Rentals,
www.rrivreworks.com

Classic Party Rentals, www.classicpartyrentals.com

Chameleon Chair, www.chameleonchair.com

LIFE IS A BEACH
Leo and Christine Wuth, hosts

Rrivre Works Event Design and Prop Rental,
www.rrivreworks.com

Classic Party Rentals, www.classicpartyrentals.com

James Hickey, www.henshallphotography.com

LOVE THAT!
Virginia Madsen, host

Classic Party Rentals, www.classicpartyrentals.com

Rrivre Works Event Design and Prop Rental,
www.rrivreworks.com

Wildflower Linen, www.wildflowerlinens.com

Sweet Lady Jane, www.sweetladyjane.com

WINE AND DINE
David and Kathy McDonald, hosts

Classic Party Rentals, www.classicpartyrentals.com

LOVE & MARRIAGE
Kevin Montgomery and Dennis Duban, hosts

Gull's Way Estate

Classic Party Rentals, www.classicpartyrentals.com

Wildflower Linen, www.wildflowerlinens.com

The Cake Studio, www.thecakestudio.us

The Lighter Side, www.specialeventlighting.com

Form Décor, www.formdecor.com

Lenetta Kidd Productions, www.lenettakiddproductions.com

Mikel Healey, www.mikelhealeyphoto.com

INDEX